James Q. Moore

THE LARGER FAITH

THE LARGER FAITH

BY

CHARLES R. BROWN

Dean of the Divinity School
Yale University

THE PILGRIM PRESS

BOSTON   CHICAGO

Printed in the United States of America

THE JORDAN & MORE PRESS
BOSTON

CONTENTS

THE POINT OF VIEW 3

I. THE BAPTIST CHURCH 11

II. THE CONGREGATIONAL CHURCH . . 29

III. THE CHURCH OF THE DISCIPLES . . 49

IV. THE EPISCOPAL CHURCH 67

V. THE LUTHERAN CHURCH 89

VI. THE METHODIST CHURCH 105

VII. THE PRESBYTERIAN CHURCH . . . 123

VIII. THE ROMAN CATHOLIC CHURCH . . 141

IX. THE UNITARIAN CHURCH 163

X. "THE UNITY OF THE SPIRIT" . . . 181

APPENDIX 191

THE POINT OF VIEW

The Point of View

This modest little volume is not an attempt at a Church History, nor is it a study in comparative sectarianism. It is an appreciation. It was written primarily for young people who are not firmly set in their own denominational preferences — they want to know the special features in the work of the various sections of the Universal Church. It was written in the interest of that better understanding and more intelligent good will among the many branches of the Church of Christ which will aid in replacing the spirit of rivalry and antagonism with the spirit of coöperation for the gaining of those ends which belong to all who follow the Master.

Our total Christianity is a very large affair. "Like a mighty army moves the Church of God." It is not all Infantry nor all Artillery nor all Cavalry nor all Air Service nor all Ambulance Corps. Each one of these arms of a common service has its own particular field of usefulness, yet the army is one.

In view of the fact that Christianity is a large and diversified movement for human betterment, it is good for every man, now and then, to get out of his own special corner of the field and take a look at the army as a whole. It is good for him to feel something of the swing and movement of these far-flung, variously formulated efforts to have righteousness bear rule. It will lift him out of that pettiness and meagerness into which the best of men fall at times and bestow upon him something of the breadth and bigness, something of the sympathy and catholicity of spirit which belong to joyous citizenship in the Kingdom of God.

It is well for any individual Christian occasionally to take some other man's gait. There are bodies of Christians which move habitually in a regular and dignified walk — the Presbyterians for example in the general quality of their church life have learned to " walk and not faint." There are others who occasionally strike a good round trot, others less conventional in their methods are accustomed to pace, while some zealous people even break into a splendid gallop.

Well and good! If they are only headed right, God be praised for this variety of movement! And for the man who on the whole strongly prefers his own particular gait, it is desirable that for an hour he should catch some other man's mood and movement — he will come back to his own place in the procession, a more limber, a more likable and a more useful Christian.

The purpose of these chapters is not in any sense controversial. If I could not find anything to write about except to make a series of ill-natured attacks upon my fellow Christians in those other camps, I should certainly lay down my pen at once.

4

There are better uses for paper and ink than to employ them in sectarian controversy. The devil is too much in evidence these days for Christians to be fighting each other when they might be fighting him.

The newspapers make much oftentimes of " the divisions of Christendom," but they know not what they say. The divisions on the face of them are many, too many, but the agreements are more numerous and ever so much more significant. The deeper meaning of the divisions themselves lies in the fact that each group of Christians, which has any sort of right to be, has made some special and distinctive contribution to "The Larger Faith."

There are narrow-minded bigots and sectarians who do not view the matter in this way. They are so taken up with the beauties of their own little cob-houses of doctrine, polity and ritual that they have no admiration left for anything outside. They have no real appreciation of the great cathedral-like structure of Christian faith and worship and service, with its nave and choir, its added transepts and out-reaching chapels, representing a long and varied process of growth.

But we may rejoice to believe that there are not many of these precious bigots left and they do not count for much even in their own sects. The theology, the polity and the worship of any one branch of the total Church are not sufficiently roomy to include all the facts of human nature,

5

to say nothing of drawing a complete circle around the divine love. In the chapters which follow I wish to stand in the presence of that larger Christianity which may well command the esteem and the allegiance of all our hearts.

I shall consider briefly nine of the leading branches of the Christian Church in this country, the Baptist, the Congregational, the Disciples, the Episcopal, the Lutheran, the Methodist, the Presbyterian, the Roman Catholic and the Unitarian Churches. I have simply arranged them in alphabetical order without any attempt to catalogue them in chronological fashion or with reference to their respective importance.

There are other branches of the Church not named here which would naturally come in for sympathetic consideration. The Reformed Church and the United Brethren have had an important and an honorable part in the religious development of America. But the general method and contribution of the Reformed Churches have been so similar to those of the Presbyterian Church, and the methods and contributions of the United Brethren so like those of the Methodists, that I have not here undertaken the separate treatment of either one. The Universalist Church rendered a vital service in modifying a harsh and arbitrary doctrine of future retribution (so widely held at the time the protest was made) and in giving courage to those who would cherish " the larger hope," but again its point of view and prevailing spirit have been closely akin to those of the Unitarian Church. In any exhaustive account of the religious forces of the nation, there are still other churches which would demand thoughtful consideration, but I have selected the nine which are named above, because they are the best known and because in my judgment each one has made some distinctive contribution to " The Larger Faith."

If we can undertake this excursion through these varied fields of Christian effort in the spirit of intellectual hospitality, we shall bring back, I trust, stirrings of sympathy, fairer judgments and refreshing outlooks upon other quarters of the infinite heaven of religious reality which will broaden and inspire us for a finer, fuller service of our common Lord.

THE BAPTIST CHURCH

Chapter I

The Baptist Church

The name " Baptist " as applied to a particular branch of the Christian Church dates back to about the year 1664. It was used to designate a certain body of Christians as indicating the peculiar emphasis they laid upon the mode and upon the proper subjects of baptism. They insisted that the literal meaning of the Greek word *Baptizo* is " to dip," and that inasmuch as baptism by the immersion of the whole body in water was common, if not universal, in Christ's day, this mode is the one acceptable mode of administering that sacrament. They also insisted that the church should be composed only of regenerate believers; and that only people sufficiently mature to make conscious acceptance of Christ as their Saviour could therefore be rightly admitted to the church through the ordinance of baptism. They did not practice the baptism of infants according to the usage of the larger part of the Church of Christ.

I shall not stop to discuss either of these claims. I feel, as the Baptists themselves feel, that baptism with water is of little importance as compared with the baptism of the Spirit. It was John the Baptist himself who said, " I indeed baptize you with water " — that was all he could do — " but One cometh after me, mightier than I, whose shoes I am not worthy to bear, He shall baptize you with the Holy Ghost and with fire." I crave for myself, as all Christians do, a fuller baptism of the Spirit that was in Him.

There are thousands of people, both in the Baptist Church and out of it, who believe as Dean Stanley did that in the first century the mode of baptism which was common if not universal may have been by immersion; and they believe also that the departure from that mode, which occurred very early and which has come to prevail so widely, may represent for colder regions where different styles of dress obtain, " the triumph of convenience and good taste over a literal attachment to ancient custom." I am not undertaking, however, to argue the differing claims as to the mode or the subjects of baptism, but rather to indicate the distinctive contribution made by each body of Christians to our total Christianity.

I

The special contribution of the Baptist Church seems to me to lie in three directions: — first, in their intense loyalty to personal conviction. Our good friends in the Baptist Church believe that Jesus Christ was baptized by immersion in the river Jordan. They believe that the early Christians were thus baptized by the apostles. Many of them regard it as essential even in this far-off land and time, that every believing Christian should be baptized in the same way. Because of their loyalty to this conviction they stand ready to make the necessary sacrifices in maintaining that mode.

This loyalty to conviction becomes oftentimes a serious handicap. In a warm country like Palestine where many of the people lived near running streams, where the loose outer garments could be readily laid aside without unseemliness, the custom of immersion was one thing. In colder countries where water must be artificially heated in tanks or where people in the country must go to ponds or to streams and in the winter season cut holes through the ice in order to perform this rite in that way, and where the style of dress is such as to involve much inconvenience and discomfort, immersion is quite another thing. " Well and good," the Baptists say— " even though we find ourselves in many cases compelled to overcome a measure of reluctance on the part of thousands of people to that mode of baptism, we believe it to be right and we gladly accept that difficulty."

However the rest of the Christian world may differ with them as to the importance of that particular mode of baptism, we cannot but admire their intense loyalty to conviction. I have been present at baptisms in country places where the candidates were driven several miles from their homes in the coldest weather, where a hole had been cut through the ice and where believers were immersed in freezing water and were then compelled to drive several miles to the nearest house to secure a change of clothing. The physical discomfort was accepted as a matter of course in no spirit of complaint but as an opportunity for bearing witness to their faith in Christ.

Let that same loyalty to conviction, that same tenacity of purpose, extend to matters more vital than the mode of baptism, as indeed it has in large measure extended among the Christians of that faith, and one can see what a power for good it may become! Let loyalty to conviction be directed to the consecration of one's powers to Christian service, to the devotion of one's means to benevolence and to the development of a sincere attachment to the church of one's choice, and it becomes at once a mighty influence for good!

The Baptists emphasize the sacredness of the individual conscience. This lies at the root of their refusal to baptize children. The helpless child must not be carried into the church and there baptized by sprinkling (or by immersion, for that matter, which would equally offend their sense of right). We must wait until the conscious moral life of this child has taken shape and has made its own choice as to the mode of baptism, until it has made a personal decision as to the whole question of Christian worship and service. " Everyone of us shall give an account of himself to God," is a favorite text with the Baptists, and their very insistence upon the right and obligation of individual judgment in all matters of religion has helped to develop that intense loyalty to personal conviction. It has been a great asset to the cause of democracy throughout the world — the right of every man to think for himself and decide for himself upon his course of action, ready at whatever cost to obey the voice of conscience within his own breast.

II

The second contribution may be found in the simplicity of their creed. For more than a century the Baptists had no formulated creed. They simply referred believers to the Bible as the only standard of faith and conduct. Even now they have no authoritative creed statements or symbols. What is known as the " New Hampshire Confession of Faith " is widely published throughout the North, and another known as the " Philadelphia Confession of Faith " is current through the South. But these statements are for instruction rather than for enforcement. They are not binding in the sense that the Thirty-nine Articles of the Episcopal Church or the Twenty-five Articles of the Methodist Church or the Westminster Confession in the Presbyterian Church are binding upon the teachers of religion in these bodies. The creed of the Baptists is the Bible, and they have not undertaken to formulate its teachings in any authoritative creed statements.

15

The Larger Faith

Two of the points which come in for special emphasis in this church are indicated in one of their favorite texts — " He that believeth and is baptized shall be saved." He that believes, not certain creed statements contained in the Thirty-nine Articles or in the Westminster Confession; he that believes on Christ, in His gospel, in His purposes for the world, and is ready to bear witness to that belief in baptism, shall be saved. The inner attitude of the moral nature toward Christ and the open confession of that attitude in baptism are the two essentials for salvation. As compared with the elaborate dogmas of some branches of the Christian Church, there is among the Baptists great simplicity of creed.

The working out of this principle can be seen in such an institution as the University of Chicago. It is one of the very few great Universities (aside from the Universities of the Roman Catholic Church) which is under denominational control. It is a Baptist institution. It was founded and handsomely endowed by a well-known Baptist layman, Mr. John D. Rockefeller. Until very recently it was required that its President should be a member of the Baptist Church and it still requires that three-fifths of the members of its governing Board shall be members of that communion. But when we come to its various Faculties, including the Faculty of the Divinity School, we find a wide range of church affiliations allowed and a great variety of theological beliefs sincerely cherished and openly taught. There is no creed but the Bible and the interpretation of the Bible according to each man's understanding of it leaves room for a large amount of personal liberty.

The very simplicity and comprehensiveness of this basis has given the Baptist Church a certain facility in securing and utilizing men of striking personality and of unconventional methods as ministers of their faith. Take two men, well known to our own generation, — one on this side of the water and one on that — Charles H. Spurgeon of London, and Russell H. Conwell of Philadelphia, both of them famous Baptist preachers.

Spurgeon preached to more people than any other man of the Nineteenth Century. He preached to seven thousand of them Sunday after Sunday in his own Tabernacle in South London. On the " Day of Humiliation " at the time of the Indian Mutiny he preached in Crystal Palace to twenty-four thousand people and his marvelous voice (without any aid from the recently invented amplifiers) enabled them all to hear his message.

His sermons were printed in pamphlets and in book form, and are being printed yet, although he has been dead for more than thirty years; and the circulation of them has extended into millions of copies. He was in no sense a scholar — he knew almost nothing about the critical study of the Bible, or of church history, or of philosophy. But " he be-

lieved what he believed, and for the man whose
main business it is to produce faith in other men
this is more valuable than all technical scholarship." He proclaimed Christ and Him crucified
with wonderful effect.

He was unconventional — he would joke in the
pulpit and shock the taste of his more sensitive
hearers. When preaching about hell and certain
other doctrines he would indulge in language so
extravagant that we would scarcely credit it did
we not find it in print in volumes published under
his own supervision. But he knew the common
people and they knew him. He won thousands
of them to Christian life and service. He accomplished results in which every thoughtful
Christian rejoices. His later life was clouded by
his feeling that the Baptist denomination was
becoming too liberal in its views on the fall of man,
the atonement, the inspiration of the Bible and
the fate of the wicked, and consequently he with-
drew from the Baptist Union. During the latter
part of his ministry he and his church stood alone,
but his bow abode in strength, and his power of
appeal was mighty.

Russell H. Conwell, whose lecture on " Acres of
Diamonds " has been given some eight thousand
times, earning for him a large amount of money,
which he has promptly put back into the philanthropic work of his own church and of his college
for working people, has been one of the most

striking figures in the modern pulpit. His work in the Temple Baptist Church in Philadelphia, especially in the educational and social facilities offered to young men and young women unable to go to college, has been greatly blessed. He has been recently honored by the award of a service medal given to him as " the most useful citizen " in the City of Brotherly Love. I could name many other outstanding figures in the Baptist pulpit but these two may serve to illustrate the principle named above.

III

The third contribution made by the Baptists has been in their strong insistence upon the entire separation of Church and State. This separation of civil and religious authority may seem to many people in this country like one of those things which goes without saying. It has not always been so and it is not so now — " the more's the pity " — in many other lands. It is for the good of both Church and State that they should move along distinct lines — lines which may indeed stretch out in the same general direction toward human well-being but they should not be made identical nor should either attempt to rule the other. " Render unto Cæsar the things which are Cæsar's " but only the things which are Cæsar's — this has been the steady contention of the Baptist in all lands and in all times.

The Larger Faith

Roger Williams, one of the early Baptist heroes in this country, was driven out of Massachusetts, not because he believed in immersion or because of any special religious tenets he held. At that time he was not even a Baptist for he was not immersed until after he went to Rhode Island. He was driven out because of his extreme individualism in insisting upon the separation of Church and State. As soon as he landed in this country he stirred up trouble by urging the Christians of Massachusetts to join in an act of public repentance for having communed with the Church of England, which was a state church. He wrote against the Massachusetts Patent, claiming that the king of England had no right to grant land to the colonists. He censured the Colony for requiring oaths from citizens on the ground that to exact an oath from an unregenerate person involved the sin of taking God's name in vain. He denied any power to the civil magistrate in matters of religious faith.

This was not acceptable to the people of Massachusetts Bay at that time. They still maintained a close relation between Church and State. Thus Roger Williams became what Theodore Roosevelt called " an undesirable citizen," and he was invited to leave as a troublesome agitator. He went to Providence, was there immersed, became a Baptist and founded Rhode Island, the first state in the Union to guarantee entire religious freedom.

It was a protest sorely needed in that day.

Massachusetts had passed laws against Baptists because of their attitude touching these matters in 1644, had imprisoned them in 1651 and banished them in 1669. This was religious persecution by civil authority, which the Baptists have always opposed. New York did the same thing and so did Virginia. The Protestant churches of Zurich, Switzerland, having just won their own liberty and still in dread of Rome, nevertheless passed an ordinance that any minister administering the rite of baptism by immersion should be drowned — with some idea of poetic justice perhaps, making " the punishment fit the crime." They actually executed that sentence against one Felix Mantz, a Baptist minister, by drowning him in the lake of Zurich.

As late as the year 1863, the new code of the State of Georgia provided in Section 1376 that " it should be unlawful for any church or society to license any slave or free person of color to preach or exhort or otherwise officiate in church meetings." This aroused the Baptists of that state. They declared in a written communication to the State Legislature that this was seizing by force the things that are God's and rendering them unto Cæsar. They insisted that the State of Georgia was undertaking to dictate to the Almighty what color his preachers should be. And they announced that even with such an enactment before their eyes they would ordain negroes to the ministry if they were godly men. They then proceeded to ordain two; and the protest of those southern Baptists became so effective that the offending section was repealed at the next session of the Legislature. The Baptists have been ready to go all lengths in their insistence upon the entire separation of Church and State.

In England at this hour John Clifford, a Baptist minister, is one of the forces to be reckoned with politically. He is a great tribune of the people, a voice for the non-conformist conscience of Great Britain. He supported Gladstone, opposed the Boer War, fought the brewers when they lined up with the Lords to oppose temperance legislation, which was sadly needed. He opposed the Education Act and allowed his own private property to be taken away from him by the Government rather than pay taxes collected by the State to support church schools. He urged the dis-establishment of the state church on the ground that the civil authorities have no right to impose upon the people the burden of supporting any form of religion by public taxation. He helped in the triumph of the Liberal Party in 1906, representing the people as against " the interests " and the hereditary aristocracy. When I was in England I heard him speak repeatedly at great public demonstrations in Hyde Park and elsewhere and I could understand how in that land of tradition, of class feeling, of close connection between Church and State, he had become a mighty influence for good by his steady insistence upon this fundamental Baptist principle of entire separation of civil and religious authority.

It was no less a man than Macaulay, a warm friend of the aristocracy and a strong supporter of the Established Church, who said, "There were many cultivated minds in England during the latter part of the Seventeenth Century but there were only two great creative minds. One of them was the author of *Paradise Lost*, and the other was the author of *Pilgrim's Progress*." The author of *Paradise Lost* was John Milton, a man born and reared in the Church of England. The author of *Pilgrim's Progress* was John Bunyan, an untitled Baptist preacher. His book became and has remained for more than two hundred years a genuine classic for the whole English-speaking world.

The history of the Baptist people in regard to missionary effort has been a curious one. When the idea of sending missionaries to foreign lands was first suggested, it split the church. The anti-missionary party said, "If God wants the heathen converted he will convert them without our help." Because of their extreme Calvinism they insisted that the efforts of the missionary societies would be "an unjustifiable encroachment upon the divine sovereignty," for God by his eternal decrees had determined from all eternity who should be saved and who should be lost. And the Baptists who held this view were split off and became a separate denomination.

But the missionary spirit grew and " the missionary Baptists " were the first in England to organize a missionary society and in 1793 William Carey went out to become one of the noblest missionaries in the history of India. In 1812 Adoniram Judson, who was a Congregationalist, was sent out by the American Board of Foreign Missions in that church but he changed his views on baptism during the voyage and upon reaching Calcutta was immersed and became a widely known and honored missionary of the Baptist denomination in Burmah. The world-wide, generous interest of the Baptist people in missionary enterprises has been a leading note in their church life for the last hundred years.

Have we not great need of these fine qualities for which the Baptist Church has been conspicuous? We have seen the liberties of free men, and the great cause of democracy threatened by the resolute attack of a mad military caste which undertook the subjugation of a whole continent in its own interest. In that government the individual was sacrificed to the State. He was not " free to think and act, free to look at fact, free to come and go " — he was only a blind and submissive cog in a machine whose wheels turned at the will of its self-appointed supervisors. Under that régime when one button was pressed the clergy danced;

when another button was pressed by the proper official the university professors danced; and when another button was pressed the state-employed servants of mercantile interests made their obeisance. It was a fearfully effective and menacing system.

That whole method jars upon the man reared in this atmosphere of freedom. " Stand fast, therefore, in the liberty wherewith Christ hath made you free! Be not entangled with the yoke of bondage. Ye have been called unto liberty, only use not liberty for an occasion to the flesh but by love serve one another."

Let every man be true, the Baptist Church would say, true to the voice within, true to his personal convictions of right and wrong, true to the American spirit of separation between Church and State, true to God, that he may enter into the full inheritance which belongs alike to every child of the Most High.

THE CONGREGATIONAL CHURCH

CHAPTER II

The Congregational Church

The Congregational Church is my own church. I was not born so — my father was a Methodist and my mother until after her marriage was a Presbyterian. But when I came to choose for myself, I felt that I would be happier and more useful in the Congregational Church which for thirty-odd years has been my spiritual home. I have written in cordial, sympathetic terms of the strong points in the other churches and of the contributions they have made to our total Christianity. In writing of my own church it would be neither fair nor honest did I not speak in the same frank way of its excellences. I trust that I may do this not in the spirit of boasting but in open recognition of any contribution which this church has made to " The Larger Faith."

The Congregational body takes its name from the fact that all power is vested in the " congregation " of the local church. Any company of Christian believers associating themselves together for the worship of God and the service of man constitute, according to this view, a complete church. This single congregation standing alone, acknowledging only Christ as the Head of all the Churches,

is competent to formulate its own creed, to arrange
its own mode of worship, to elect and set apart its
own officers, pastor, deacons and the like, to manage its own affairs as to sacraments, benevolences
and other matters of church life, to receive and
dismiss members, by the vote of the congregation.
It does all this looking to no outside authority
whatsoever, bishops, presbyteries, conferences or
assemblies, but only to such guidance as may come
by the Spirit of the unseen Head of the Church.
All earthly authority inheres in the congregation,
and consequently such a church is called a " Congregational Church."

I

The four main contributions which this branch of
Christ's Church seems to have made to our total
Christianity are these — first, its high confidence
in a pure democracy. Its form of polity is " government of the people, by the people and for the
people." It trusts the people to manage their own
spiritual affairs. It trusts any group of Christian
people, large or small, rural or urban, simple or
cultured, who have been led to organize themselves
under the leadership of Christ into a Christian
church.

The whole idea of dependence upon some set of
officers placed over them to tell them what they
shall believe in their creeds, what they shall say in
their prayers and their other forms of worship, who

their pastor shall be and how he shall be set apart to that office, is foreign to their method. They would no more accept it than they would accept the idea that domestic life needs some such official supervision. "We are a family in the Lord," they say — "One is our Master, even Christ, and all we are brethren." We acknowledge no other authority, save Christ as the Head of the Church, in questions of creed, ritual, ministry or service,— all these matters are to be determined by each church family for itself.

"From within outward, from beneath upward, is the direction of life," Dr. Storrs once said, "in the spiritual no less than in the physical world. To undertake to reverse this process in church life seems to us as unreasonable as trying to set a growing tree on its branches instead of its roots." Power goes up, not down, all governments deriving their just powers from the consent of the governed.

One can readily understand how such a form of church government came to be. It was a protest against the monarchical spirit in religion. The principle of local self-government indicated that the unit of sovereignty in religious matters should be the local congregation of believers. The Congregational polity, therefore, is not monarchical in that it refuses to be governed by bishops. It is not a representative form of government in that it declines the rule of elders. It is a pure democracy

31

in that it commits all power directly into the hands of the people.

Whatever is done in the Congregational Church is done directly by the vote of the congregation. If a pastor is to be called, if some young man is to be ordained to the ministry, if a change is to be made in the creed, if any innovation is desired in the ritual or the forms of worship, if a new member is to be received, if a member is to be dismissed to some other church, if money is to be given in benevolence, if anything whatsoever which pertains to church life is to be done, no outside authority has anything to say in the matter. In every one of these instances the initiative is taken by the congregation. The pastor has no authority to issue a letter of transfer to a member desiring to unite with another church, as would be the case in the Episcopal or the Methodist Church — this, too, must be done by the vote of the congregation, and the letter of transfer will be signed by the Clerk of the Church.

In the Congregational Church the pastor himself does not belong to a separate class. He is not a member of a conference, as the Methodist pastor is, or of a diocese as the rector in an Episcopal Church is, or of a Presbytery, according to the usage of the Presbyterians. He is a member of the church he serves, uniting with it by letter from the church with which he was last connected, like any other member. He is pastor, not because he belongs to

32

a separate priestly or preaching order, but by virtue of his election to that office by the votes of his fellow members of the congregation.

It is the idea of the New England town meeting incorporated into church life. It is pure democracy, in that authority is not handed down from above, nor delegated to certain chosen representatives, but retained throughout in the hands of the people themselves. It is a form of polity which is shared by the Disciples of Christ and by the Baptist and the Unitarian Churches, but the Congregationalists were the first to practice it, and they have placed upon it peculiar emphasis.

It is their belief that the earliest churches of apostolic times enjoyed this simple form of government. We do not find in the New Testament any one central authority controlling all the churches, but each congregation proceeding upon its way with the words, " It seemed good to the Holy Ghost and to us," as a sufficient sanction for its action. We find references to " the church at Jerusalem," " the church of Antioch," " the churches of Asia," and " the churches of Cilicia," indicating the common usage. In similar fashion the Congregational people do not ordinarily use the term " The Congregational Church " as comprising all the people of their faith — they speak of " The Congregational Churches," for each congregation is a church in itself. In committing all authority as to creed, ritual, and government into the hands of the local congregation, they assert their confidence in the value and efficiency of pure democracy. In these recent years when God seems to have been saying with renewed emphasis, " I am tired of kings " one can see at a glance the value of this particular contribution to " The Larger Faith. "

II

The second contribution lies in their intellectual breadth. The Congregational attitude in matters of belief may be indicated by these familiar words, — " In essentials, unity; in non-essentials, liberty; in all things, charity." We would not place a man in a Congregational pulpit who was an atheist, or one who denied the validity of those principles of right living contained in the words of Christ, or one who set at naught what are universally regarded among Christians as the eternal verities of the spiritual world. But upon the basis of certain great fundamentals we build a church life which is characterized by large intellectual hospitality. We have had among our laymen, and in our ministry, men of very conservative views — Joseph Cook, a kind of arch-defender of old-fashioned orthodoxy, was to the day of his death a Congregational minister. We have also men of exceedingly liberal and radical opinions — Lyman Abbott, editor of the *Outlook*, was an honored and useful Congregational minister. John Robinson urged the Pilgrims when they were about to sail for America, to " believe that God had much more light to fall from His Holy Word," and they tried to live with their eyes and minds open for that fuller light.

We find it more easy to maintain this theological hospitality because we have no formulated articles of religion or creed statements, which are universally binding as are the Articles of Religion, or the Westminster Confession in the Episcopal, the Methodist and the Presbyterian Churches. Each local congregation formulates its own creed. If the pastor is in agreement with the creed of his own church, and if his teaching is acceptable to that congregation to which he ministers, no outside authority can disturb him.

Touching things fundamental, we maintain a general consensus of belief among our churches, sufficient for harmony of action, by the second principle of our polity, known as " the fellowship of the churches." Each church is expected to live on terms of fellowship with its sister churches. In the decision of vital questions each church is encouraged to ask counsel from other churches, and in turn to give such advice when it is sought by neighboring churches through what are known as " Ecclesiastical Councils." It is understood, however, throughout, that this relation is advisory and not mandatory. Thus the churches living in fellowship with one another maintain an adequate doctrinal agreement among themselves, each one formulating and adopting its own particular creed, to secure that harmony of action which has been ours for centuries.

We strive to exhibit this breadth, not only in questions of doctrine, but in matters of Christian usage. We prescribe no form of worship, as certain other branches of the Church do. If any congregation wishes to adopt a full-orbed liturgical service as the church served by W. E. Orchard in London has done, with prayers, collects and lessons all prescribed, it has that privilege. If some other congregation wishes to observe the utmost simplicity, it enjoys the same liberty. We prescribe no fixed form for any of the Christian rites — we leave the mode of baptism to the conscience of the candidate. In my own ministry I have sprinkled hundreds of people, and I have also immersed a goodly number, who preferred that mode of baptism.

We build no barriers, doctrinal or otherwise, around the Communion Table. We cordially invite " all who love our Lord Jesus Christ in sincerity and truth " to commune with us whatever may be their church affiliations or their particular theological beliefs. In matters of doctrine we are happy in having men of conservative temper among us — we do not wish to make them uncomfortable because of their conservatism. We are happy in having liberals — we believe that wherever they are sincere followers of Christ, the Church

He founded should be roomy enough to make them also at home. As we view it the ultimate test of Christian discipleship is not theological theory, but love and devotion to the Master — " By this shall all men know that ye are my disciples, if ye love one another."

III

The third contribution may be found in the special emphasis laid upon education by Congregationalists everywhere. I am not intimating that the Congregational Church stands alone in this — all branches of the Church stand for intellectual training, but its contribution to the work of higher education in this country was the earliest and has been in certain ways the most remarkable. The Pilgrim Fathers, a little company of empty-handed people in a new and wild country, landed at Plymouth in 1620. They were compelled to labor " in hunger and cold, in weariness and painfulness." Yet in exactly sixteen years from the time they landed on that bleak coast, out of their penury, they founded Harvard College, the oldest and perhaps the most influential institution for higher education in America.

The Congregationalists founded Harvard and Yale, Bowdoin and Dartmouth, Williams and Amherst, Oberlin and Beloit, Grinnell, Washburn, Carleton, Colorado, Whitman, Pomona and other colleges to the number of fifty-six in the United

States — a number out of all proportion to their size as a denomination, for they are not one of the larger sects. For the higher education of women the Congregationalists founded Wellesley and Smith, Mount Holyoke and Mills Colleges, that women might be the intellectual companions and associates of men in all the wider interests of their lives. They began this work of higher education primarily that they might have an educated ministry, but they did it likewise that young men and maidens might receive their training under the stimulus and guidance of Christian ideals.

The one man who has influenced the theological thinking of experts in this country more than any other, the man who ranked as the greatest theologian of the Eighteenth Century in any country, Jonathan Edwards, was a Congregational minister at Northampton, Massachusetts. The two men in America who did more, perhaps, than any other two who could be named to influence the popular mind to accept more reasonable and more helpful views of Christian doctrine, Horace Bushnell, with his emphasis upon Christian nurture, and Henry Ward Beecher, in his mighty protest against the more awful aspects of Calvinism, were both Congregational pastors.

Because of this emphasis upon the value of college and seminary training this denomination, although one of the smaller sects, has produced a splendid list of great preachers in America —

The Congregational Church

Beecher and Bushnell, William M. Taylor and Richard S. Storrs, Lyman Abbott and Theodore T. Munger, Washington Gladden and Amory H. Bradford, George A. Gordon and Charles E. Jefferson, S. Parkes Cadman and Frank W. Gunsaulus! They have been great preachers, reaching the ears, the minds and the hearts of the many by the power of their message conveyed, as it has been, through the medium of trained and consecrated personality. The very quality of our church life freed from the trammels of officialism and mechanism has encouraged the development of strong, stimulating, independent personality — and this coupled with an emphasis upon training through education has forwarded the growth of preaching of a higher order.

The Congregational Church has been a teaching church. It has sought to lead men to know Him who said, " I am the truth, and ye shall know the truth and the truth shall make you free " from that which hinders life. It has produced a long list of noble and useful educators — Mark Hopkins at Williams, of whom Garfield said, " Mark Hopkins at one end of a log and myself at the other would be college enough for me "; Timothy Dwight, Noah Porter and Theodore Wolsey of Yale, Austin Phelps and Edwards Park of Andover, Charles G. Finney of Oberlin and William J. Tucker of Dartmouth, William Dewitt Hyde of Bowdoin, Daniel C. Gilman of Johns Hopkins, Cyrus Northrup of Minnesota, James B. Angell of Michigan, Mary Lyon of Mt. Holyoke and Alice Freeman Palmer of Wellesley,— all of them Congregationalists. If you would find their monuments, look not in some place of cold marble — look at the lives which caught from them the spirit of noble living and of useful service.

The two most widely read religious periodicals in this country, the *Outlook* and the *Independent*, were both founded by Congregationalists and both of them for many years had Congregational ministers as their managing editors.

The same emphasis on education has enabled this branch of the Church to produce an unusual number of great hymn writers — Isaac Watts and Philip Doddridge, who set the praise of the fathers to music, were both Congregationalists. In more recent years Ray Palmer, whose " My Faith Looks up to Thee " has been sung everywhere, Timothy Dwight, Leonard Bacon and Washington Gladden have contributed hymns which now belong to the universal Church. Lowell Mason, who for eighty years gave his strength and taste to the improvement of church music in such a way as to be called " the father of American church music," was a lifelong member of the Congregational body.

It has been a teaching church and while it may have lacked some of the warmth and fervor of the Methodists, while it may have been less tenacious of its doctrinal positions than the Presbyterian

Church, it has effectively construed the religious life in terms of education, seeking to lead men to know the truth which makes men wise unto salvation. Time would fail me to tell of all of the less famous colleges and academies established by the people of this church, north, south, east and west, each gathering its pupils to confer upon them those benefits which belong both to the life that now is and to the life which is to come.

IV

In the fourth place, this Church has been notable for its missionary spirit and zeal. The first missionary organization in this country to send the gospel to non-Christian lands was the " American Board of Foreign Missions," which resulted from the Hay Stack prayer-meeting at Williams College more than a century ago. The American Board remains to this day in the personality of its missionaries and in the high quality of its work one of the leading missionary societies of the world. The largest gifts per capita for the work of foreign missions for many years were made by the Congregationalists, excepting only that little group of Christians known as Moravians, whose warm and generous missionary zeal has exceeded that of any other church in Christendom.

And some of the most useful and famous missionaries in the foreign field have been of this faith. In many lands their work has been nothing less

than epoch-making — John Eliot, the apostle to
the Indians and Cyrus Hamlin in Turkey, Hiram
Bingham of Hawaii and Robert A. Hume of India,
Arthur H. Smith of China and James H. deForest
of Japan, men with the hearts of saints and the
minds of statesmen! They wrought righteousness
and obtained the promises, subdued kingdoms and
put to flight armies of evil. As a result of their
labors, men have seen the Kingdom of God coming
with power in many a land.

This Church was the first to organize a foreign
missionary society and the first also to organize a
home missionary society for the evangelization of
our own land. The work of the home missionary
is less romantic and picturesque but he has gone
to the lumber camps, the mining towns and to the
lonely communities in the midst of the great wide
ranches to make known to men the good news of
life eternal. We had an " Iowa Band " which
came out from Andover Seminary and their names
are written across the moral life of that great state
in the Middle West to stay. We had a " Yale
Band " in the State of Washington and they carried
the finest traditions of that honored university to
engrave them upon the eager, restless life of the
great Northwest. The Spirit said " Go," and
they went — and all those regions which have
profited by the labors of cultured, consecrated men
rise up to-day and call them blessed.

The Congregational Church was the first to

undertake the education of the freedmen at the close of the Civil War — a comparison of statistics a few years ago showed that it had put more money at that time into Christian schools for the negroes of the South than all the other denominations combined. It was the first to introduce Christian education in Utah, making it a potent instrument there to offset the influence of Mormonism.

Its scholars have taken high place in making translations of the Scriptures into foreign languages for missionary work. Hiram Bingham reduced to writing the entire language of the Gilbert Islanders in Micronesia and made a translation of the entire Bible for their instruction. John S. Chandler utilized his seven years of training at Yale and his thorough knowledge of the vernacular to compile the standard Lexicon of the Tamil language for the people of southern India. Twenty-seven languages in all, have been reduced to writing by missionaries of the American Board and one hundred and eighty translations of the Bible into other tongues have been made by their hands and brains for the extension of the influence of the gospel of Christ.

With all its intellectual breadth (which has sometimes disturbed our more conservative brethren), with all its apparent lack of close-knit organization, the missionary spirit of the Congregational body has been so real and so warm that it has been an evangelizing church. How many of the great

historic revivals and of the mighty leaders in widespread religious movements have come from this
branch of Christ's Church! Jonathan Edwards
more than any other man was responsible for " the
great awakening " in the Eighteenth Century.
Charles G. Finney of Oberlin was the one man who
did more than any other to promote the religious
awakening which came in the decades preceding the
Civil War. Dwight L. Moody was regarded as the
most successful evangelist in the last third of the
Nineteenth Century. In noble evangelism it would
be difficult to name three men who have accomplished more for our country than Edwards,
Finney and Moody, all of them lifelong Congregationalists. The work of these men was not mere
noise and froth, creating a nine-days' wonder by
eccentric, sensational methods and then leaving the
community cold. It was the honest, effective
enlisting of men and women in the open, active
service of Christ. Of that sort of evangelism we
cannot have too much.

This branch of the Church has furnished other
widely known religious leaders — Francis E. Clark,
founder and head of the Christian Endeavor
movement, has been all these years a Congregational minister. R. J. Campbell of London while
he remained a Congregationalist led one of the
significant religious movements of the Twentieth
Century. However we may disagree with some of
his theology, or disapprove some of his peculiar

methods, he was a force to be reckoned with. Other leaders whose later work may seem less satisfying illustrate the power of this branch of the Church to develop leadership. Benjamin Fay Mills, for many years a most successful evangelist, was ordained as a Congregational minister, and for a long time was a member with us. Mrs. Mary Baker G. Eddy, the founder of Christian Science, was the product and in early life a member of our branch of the Church. Its missionary spirit and its intellectual breadth have combined to give the Congregational body a certain genius for the development of widely influential religious leaders. Its men and women, strong and free, constantly compelled to manage their own affairs, have had a way of moving to the front.

It has shown the same missionary zeal in all the great reforms. The real beginning of the temperance movement in America which has now taken shape in the form of an Amendment to the Federal Constitution, dates from a series of sermons preached against the evil of intemperance in New England by Lyman Beecher at a time when tippling was common both with the ministers and the laity of the evangelical churches. In the early agitation against slavery few more conspicuous figures are to be found than those of Henry Ward Beecher, Leonard Bacon and Harriet Beecher Stowe. The first social settlement to transplant living Christianity into the less favored section of a large city

by sending a group of cultured men and women to
live there was the Andover House in Boston —
now the South End House — taking its name
originally from the fact that Andover Theological
Seminary stood behind it. One of the most useful
men in that work today is Graham Taylor in the
Chicago Commons, a professor in one of our Semi-
naries. The earliest "Institutional Churches"
to achieve success along the line of a more varied
form of service to the community, were Berkeley
Temple in Boston, the Tabernacle Church in Jersey
City and the Fourth Congregational Church of
Hartford. Washington Gladden, Raymond Rob-
bins and other well known Congregationalists have
been leaders in the high task of making thorough,
intelligent application of the principles of the Sermon on the Mount to the social and industrial
conditions under which men live. In every form
of good work that same missionary zeal, cherished
and handed on, has found useful expression.

The real essence of Congregationalism is not to
be found in a certain type of church polity, nor in
an authoritative creed statement, for it has none,
nor in a prescribed form of ritual, for its modes of
worship vary widely — the real essence of the
Pilgrim faith is to be found in a certain sense of
freedom and of fellowship in the Spirit of Christ.
One is our Master and in serving Him we are all
brothers.

THE CHURCH OF THE DISCIPLES

CHAPTER III

The Church of the Disciples

In the latter part of the Eighteenth Century, in the north of Ireland, two men lived, father and son, Thomas Campbell and Alexander Campbell. They were Presbyterian ministers, belonging to that section of the Church known as "The Seceders." They were deeply religious men and, possessing in generous measure the qualities of leadership, they were destined to play a large part in an important religious movement here in this newer section of the world.

Thomas Campbell had been educated in Glasgow University and in Divinity Hall. He was scholarly, lovable, devout, and preëminently a man of peace. His home was a center of religious instruction and devotion, and his parish is said to have been the most exemplary in that whole region. He saw the evils of a narrow sectarianism, and he was earnestly desirous of promoting the spirit of Christian unity.

He was in frail health at that time and in the hope of gaining physical benefit, he emigrated in 1807 to the United States. He brought with him his credentials as a Presbyterian pastor and at a meeting of the Synod in Philadelphia, he was cordially received and recommended to the Presbytery of Chartiers, located in western Pennsylvania. Here he was assigned to a field of labor and began

49

The Larger Faith

his active ministry in this country as a pastor of
The Seceder Church.

He found in that new community numbers of
excellent church people, some of them long cherished friends from his native land. He entered into
joyous fellowship with them, ministering to them in
spiritual things. He was sent on a missionary tour
through western Pennsylvania to preach the gospel
and to administer the sacrament to the scattered
Seceders in that thinly populated region. He found
communicants of other Presbyterian bodies who
had not been enjoying the privileges of the Lord's
Supper. His heart went out to them in ready
sympathy and he openly invited them all to partici-
pate in the communion services.

This action gave offence to the stricter party
in The Seceder Church. Mr. Campbell was brought
before his Presbytery to be questioned and a vote
of censure was passed condemning him for the
practice of a more inclusive fellowship of Christians
at the table of the Lord. He appealed to the Synod,
hoping that the vote of censure would be revoked.
The Synod reviewed the case, and while it found
some irregularities in the action of the Presbytery,
the vote of censure was affirmed. This was the beginning of the separation of the Campbells from the
Presbyterian Church where they had been reared.

Thomas Campbell's withdrawal from the Seceders did not interrupt in any way his labors as a
minister of Christ. While the churches of his former

faith were not open to him, he preached in private houses, in groves and wherever opportunity might offer. In this way a considerable number of people who sympathized with his spirit and method were brought into a certain fellowship of Christian effort. A conference was arranged in a private house near Washington, Pennsylvania. Mr. Campbell opened the meeting with prayer, invoking the blessing of God and the divine guidance of the Holy Spirit upon their deliberations. Growing out of this conference there came, at a meeting held later on the head waters of Buffalo Creek, in August, 1809, the formation of what was known as " The Christian Association of Washington."

The organization of another sect or denomination of Christians did not at that time lie within the minds of these earnest people. They were not detaching themselves from the churches to which they owed allegiance. The general purpose of the movement was expressed in what is known as " The Declaration and Address " written by Thomas Campbell himself, which came to be the *magna charta* of the Disciple movement. The instrument is too long to be quoted here in its entirety, but the spirit of it has been accurately summarized by William T. Moore in his " History of the Disciples of Christ." " Our desire for ourselves and for our brethren would be, that rejecting human opinions and the inventions of men as of any authority, we might cease from further contentions, returning to and holding fast by the original standard, taking the divine Word alone for our rule, the Holy Spirit for our teacher and guide to lead us into all the truth, and Christ alone for our salvation, that by so doing we may be at peace among ourselves and follow peace with all men and holiness without which no man shall see the Lord."

Upon the basis of this " Declaration and Address " the leaders of the movement continued their work. Men and women were being won to Christ and believers were being built up in faith and hope and love. In spite of the emphasis upon Christian union, however, " The Christian Association of Washington " was gradually taking shape as a separate church. Thomas Campbell was grieved when he was accused of starting another religious denomination at a time when sectarianism was even more of a hindrance to the work of Christ in the world than it is today. He insisted that no such purpose was in his heart, that his whole aim was to heal the divisions of Christendom rather than to multiply them. And in line with that determination he decided to apply to the Synod of Pittsburg for membership in the Presbyterian Church. He wished to disclaim in the most positive way any intention of starting another sect.

He therefore made formal application in October, 1810, for " Christian and ministerial communion " with the Synod of Pittsburg. He appeared before the Synod and gave a clear, frank statement of his own religious position. His application was care-fully considered and was denied. The Synod made answer in these terms, " It was not for any immoral-ity in practice but for expressing his belief that there are some opinions taught in our Confession of Faith which are not founded in the Bible, for declar-ing that the administration of baptism to infants is not authorized by scriptural precept or example, for encouraging his son to preach the gospel without any regular authority and for opposing creeds and confessions as injurious to the cause of religion, that the Synod deemed it improper to grant his request."

Just at this time Alexander Campbell, the son of Thomas Campbell, entered actively into the further development of this movement. He came from Ireland to the United States in the year 1809. He approved of his father's course and he threw himself earnestly into the work of making the principles announced in the " Declaration and Address " widely known.

Alexander Campbell was a man of less concilia-tory spirit and much more aggressive than his father. He moved about through the states of West Virginia, Ohio, Pennsylvania, and Kentucky and engaged in theological debates and in pro-claiming his convictions with incisiveness and vigor. In his celebrated debate with Robert Owen " he spoke for twelve hours with only such slight interruptions as were demanded for rest and refresh-

ment." He engaged in a mighty discussion with
Archbishop Purcell in the city of Cincinnati over
the respective positions of the Disciples movement
and the Roman Catholic Church. He conducted
a debate with Nathan L. Rice of the Presbyterian
Church in Lexington, Kentucky, which extended
through eighteen days, taking up the general subject of baptism, of conversion and sanctification
and the tendency and influence of human creeds.
He started a new monthly magazine called " The
Millenial Harbinger " to contend earnestly for
what he believed to be " the faith once for all
delivered to the saints." He belonged to the
church militant and he waged an aggressive and
incessant warfare against what he regarded as
human error and sinfulness.

How far away from that whole mood and method
have we moved in these days, Presbyterians,
Methodists, Baptists, Disciples and everybody
else! The Christian world rests its weight in these
days, not so much upon the proper formulation of
theological belief, as upon the expression of spiritual
impulse in useful action. It places its emphasis not
so much upon the particular opinions men cherish
as upon the utterance of their convictions in kindly
service. It would be well-nigh impossible to induce
the great leaders of any of the Churches to engage
in these times in such extended discussion of their
theological differences and it would be altogether
impossible to induce the patient people to listen

to such presentations for twelve hours, to say nothing of lending their ears to such contentions for eighteen days. The first and great commandment is not " Thou shalt know " — it is " Thou shalt love." On the love we show for God and for man hangs our whole case.

Early in his ministry in this country Alexander Campbell became acquainted with Margaret Brown, whose home was in Brooke County, West Virginia. Their friendship soon ripened into affection and in 1811 they were married by a Presbyterian minister. They made their home on Buffalo Creek at the site of the little town of Bethany. Here Alexander Campbell lived for half a century! Here Bethany College was established and he became its first and honored President, holding this position to the close of his life! Here his curious octagonal study, entirely detached from the rest of his house, stands to this day! Here he was buried in that beautiful cemetery which has done so much to make Bethany one of the shrines and sacred places for all the Disciples of Christ.

I

The distinctive contributions made by the Disciples to our total Christianity seem to be:

First, an intense denominational consciousness! It would be difficult to name any other branch of the Protestant Church which has such a definite, loyal, close-knit, insistent feeling of fellowship.

The Larger Faith

In a somewhat more limited sense than that intended by the Master, his words may well be applied to this portion of His Church, " By this shall all men know that ye are my disciples, if ye have love one to another." The Disciples love one another, work for each other, protect each other and seek in countless ways to advance one another's interests.

This spirit where it is not wisely directed may easily have the defect of its virtues. It may lead to a narrow or bigoted clannishness. It may permit or even encourage the spirit of proselyting from other communions which are not held in the same high esteem. It may show itself unmindful of that fraternal consideration suggested by the Master where he gave his own gracious recognition to other sheep which are not of this fold.

But this is not a necessary part of that intense loyalty to one's own faith. Where can we find a more consistent, winsome and effective promoter of the spirit of Christian unity than Peter Ainslie, one of the outstanding leaders among the Disciples, for more than twenty-five years the honored and successful pastor of that great church of their faith in the city of Baltimore?

This profound denominational consciousness and this intense loyalty to the people of their own communion have gone far in enabling the Disciples to demonstrate the fact that a religious body can remain united and efficient without the aid of any

man-made creed. Their basis of agreement in having no creed statement but the Bible has been
called " A rope of sand." But by their steadfast
adherence to Christ, their basis of union has been
anything but fleeting sand — it has been like the
house of the wise man which was built upon the
rock of obedience to the great Head of the Church.
The deep denominational consciousness of these
Christians has served to hold them together in a
splendid unity of purpose.

II

The second distinctive contribution would lie
in the constant maintenance of an active evangelistic spirit. There are other branches of the Christian Church, the Methodists, the Baptists, the
United Brethren, which have shown throughout
their history a healthy spirit of evangelism. But
with them it has been more often a thing of times
and of seasons. There have come periods of
refreshing, seasons of blessing, special revival
efforts, when multitudes of those who were in
process of being saved were added to the Church.

The Disciples maintain almost without interrup-
tion the purpose, the methods and the achievements of evangelistic effort. It is their custom at
each service on the Lord's Day to " open the doors
of the church," as they say, to give opportunity
then and there at the close of each service for any
persons present to declare by coming forward their

desire to confess Christ and to become members of His Church. The minister in preparing and in preaching his sermons, the people in praying for the divine blessing to rest upon the service in which they are engaged, have it constantly in mind that the hour will find its climax in the invitation for those who would find peace to their souls to take their stand on the Lord's side. This very expectation strengthens the faith of pastor and people alike in the power of direct appeal.

This is one reason why this branch of the Church has grown so rapidly. It was celebrating its centennial anniversary in this country only yesterday, yet it has already enrolled upon the list of its members more than a million and a half followers of Christ. It is not a static but a dynamic church. It would have men come to a knowledge of the truth, and at once declare it in action. It is forever saying, " Behold I set before you this day a blessing and a curse, life and death. Therefore choose life." And its word is with power. It has written a noble record of steady and effective evangelism.

III

The third distinctive contribution may be found in the emphasis which the Disciples place upon apostolic custom. The famous dictum of Thomas Campbell, "Where the Scriptures speak we speak, where the Scriptures are silent we are silent," was as he insisted a direct return to what was apostolic. He discarded the practice of infant baptism, not upon any claim that it could not be employed to the edification of the church, but upon the ground that no clear instances of bringing infants of days to the apostles to be baptized could be found in the Bible.

He insisted upon baptism by immersion only, not upon the grounds of taste or of convenience or of the spiritual impressiveness of the rite administered in this particular way — he insisted upon immersion solely upon the ground that this was the mode of baptism practiced in the church of the apostles. He and his son had not been so baptized when they first became the leaders of the new movement, and it was an impressive scene when upon that memorable day in June, 1812, Thomas Campbell and his wife, Alexander Campbell and his wife and sister, with three others, were immersed in Buffalo Creek by Elder Luce of the Baptist Church.

It is the firm belief of the Disciples that in the early Church the taking of bread and wine in the name of Christ at the Lord's table, was a stated observance in the worship of every Lord's Day. It has proved to be a potent means of fellowship. " The meeting together once a week around the Lord's table and remembering His sacrificial death for their sins has had a comforting and a strongly uniting influence on the Disciples. In the presence of the emblems which show forth the sufferings and death of their divine Lord, they have found an irresistible bond of union and a cementing power which can come from nowhere else."

In the choice of a name they have shown the same attitude. This branch of the Church was popularly known for a long time as " The Campbellite Church." This was not acceptable to the Disciples themselves, however great might be their appreciation of the service rendered by Thomas and Alexander Campbell. They would not have their church bear the name of any man. There were many among them who favored the idea of having their denomination known simply as " The Christian Church " but wiser heads among them recognized that this would savor of arrogance and bigotry, as implying that the rest of us who follow Christ are not Christians. They would accept no name, however, which was not scriptural and apostolic. The legal name of this branch of Christ's Church therefore stands as " The Disciples of Christ."

The very name is an asset in itself. " The disciples were first called Christians at Antioch." The " disciples "! The word " disciple " comes from the Latin word " discere," to learn. The learners, the pupils, those who have by their own choice and act placed themselves directly and permanently under the tuition of the Master, are called Christians. The church is a place, not for finished scholars in the art of living, not for post-graduates who have already taken their doctors' degrees in goodness — the church is a place for learners and pupils, those who become as little children that they may enter the kingdom of Heaven. At Antioch and everywhere the people " called Christians " are the pupils of Him who is " the way and the truth and the life."

This same emphasis upon apostolic method has influenced the Disciples in defining the true object of faith. " I know whom " — not *what* but *whom* — " I have believed and I am persuaded that He is able to keep that which I have committed unto Him." The man who knows " whom " he has believed is a man of faith, even though he may not feel quite sure as to what he believes at every point. He can move ahead serene and undaunted by the power of his faith.

" Dost thou believe on the Son of God? " was the question addressed by Jesus Himself to the inquirer. It was not, " What do you believe? " And the inquirer's answer was, " Who is he, Lord, that I might believe on him? " The Disciples have steadily insisted that there is a vital difference between faith and opinion. Faith is the mood, the bearing, the response of the soul to Christ, giving substance to all the great things which are hoped for. Opinion is a state of mind while faith is an attitude of heart. From first to last the " faith " enjoined upon men in the gospel of Christ is personal rather than doctrinal.

The absence of carefully formulated creed statements has allowed and encouraged a goodly measure of intellectual liberty among the Disciples. The conservatives and the liberals alike are "called Christians " because they are the pupils and followers of the Lord Christ. Alexander Campbell himself, though he lived and died before the modern methods of historical Biblical interpretation had been introduced, in many ways anticipated the Higher Criticism in his insistence upon " Dispensational truth." He spoke of the " starlight age " and the " moonlight age " and the " sunlight age " in spiritual insight. He drew a firm line of demarcation between the law and the gospel, the old dispensation and the new. He placed a very different appraisal upon the Old Testament scriptures from that accorded to the New Testament. " We are not under Moses," he would say, " but under Christ." To his scholarly, discriminating mind the claim that " the whole Bible is the infallible word of God from lid to lid and all alike inerrant," Leviticus or Luke, Judges or John, would have been abhorrent. He believed that in the Bible as elsewhere it is first the blade, then the ear and then still later the fully ripened corn.

The Disciples do not object to the publishing and interpreting of the teaching of the Scriptures as they may bear upon any subject whatsoever of faith or duty for the purpose of instruction and education. They protest against the use of any such statements as a condition of fellowship. " It must be apparent to anyone that it is unreasonable to require children or men of undisciplined mind to subscribe to abstract statements laboriously prepared by trained thinkers as conditions of membership in Christ's Holy Church." They would have all men stand fast in the liberty wherewith Christ, through their personal trust in Him, has made them free.

When the Disciples celebrated their Centennial in 1909 in Pittsburg, the crowning feature of the whole Convention was the communion service held in the afternoon of the Lord's Day. The sacrament was celebrated in Forbes Field and thirty thousand communicants assembled to partake together of the Lord's Supper. In the whole history of the Protestant Church it was in all probability the largest communion service ever held. One hundred elders served at the tables and five hundred deacons served the great congregation with the bread and the wine of remembrance. The elders led in the words of thanksgiving and the voice of the people in praise and prayer was like the sound of many waters. When the vast congregation arose and lifted their hearts in devotion, as they sang together those words from " Nearer My God to Thee," it was a time of blessing and honor and glory and power and wisdom and might. It was an impressive fulfillment of that great word of our Lord, " And I, if I be lifted up from the earth, will draw all men unto me."

THE EPISCOPAL CHURCH

CHAPTER IV

The Episcopal Church

The full legal title of the Episcopal Church tells us something of its character and of its history. The Protestant Episcopal Church in the United States of America! This title distinguishes it from that Church which acknowledges the supremacy of the Pope at Rome — it is a " Protestant " Church. It is a church governed by bishops — an " episcopal " church. It is likewise a branch of a still older church, the Church of England — it is The Protestant Episcopal Church " in the United States of America."

It is a long and somewhat awkward title. Many attempts have been made by the General Convention to have the name changed. Some of the loyal adherents of this communion have wished to drop the word " protestant " on the ground that the Episcopal Church is a part of " The Holy Catholic Church." There are others who would have been glad to have it called " The American Church." But this has been opposed by the broader-minded Episcopalians on the ground that such a designation would seem bigoted, inasmuch as the Episcopal Church is neither the oldest nor the largest nor perhaps the most widely useful of all the Churches in America. To call it " The American Church " would be claiming for it altogether too much. It remains, therefore, The Protestant Episcopal Church.

I

Now the three main contributions made by this Church to " The Larger Faith " are in my judgment these: First, the value of system. " Let all things be done decently and in order," that is to say, with good taste and in some systematic way. This is one of the fundamental principles of that communion. In the Episcopal Church nothing is left at loose ends or dependent upon some snap judgment taken on the spur of the moment. It has its three orders of ministers, bishops, priests and deacons with the duties and privileges of each order carefully defined. It has its wardens and vestrymen among the laity. Its many societies are all carefully organized. It understands fully the importance of sound method.

In the conduct of its worship, the individual minister is not left to work out his own personal preferences or perhaps his ill-considered eccentricities. The Church puts into his hands " The Book of Common Prayer," indicating exactly what he is to say when he is leading the devotions of his people. Here are the Scripture lessons which are to be read, chapter and verse, on each day of the year! Here is the Church Year with the Gospel and the Epistle for each Sunday, outlining a kind of general program for the minister's sermons! Here is what the choir is to sing — the singers are not left free to introduce, as some choirs unhappily have done, any piece of pious doggerel set to religious rag-time or some love song with sacred words put to it. Here are the Te Deum, the Venite, the Magnificat, the Benedictus, the Nunc Dimittis and all the other offices of the church, holding the music of worship up to a high and dignified standard! "Let all things be done decently and in order," — and nothing is ever done in any other way in the Episcopal Church.

The Church Year itself, following in its lessons the main events of Christ's life, is a fine illustration of the value of system. When the first of December comes, the season of Advent leads the people to think about the power of the Scriptures, the value of the ministry and the preparation for the coming of the Messiah. Then the Christmas season leads them to think upon the nativity of Christ, the mystery of childhood, the duty of parents, the dignity of human life, as taught by the doctrine of the Incarnation. Then comes Epiphany and they follow the Wise-men with their gifts and the larger appeal of Christ's message.

Then later in the Church Year comes Lent, with its teaching of self-denial, of humility, and of separation from worldly pleasures for the deepening of the devotional life. Then comes Palm Sunday with the Triumphal Entry of Christ into the cities of men, with the assertion of his Kingship over all their varied interests. Then comes Good Friday when the people are summoned to stand before the Cross, witnessing the glory of sacrifice and meditating upon the reconciliation there accomplished between God and man. Then Easter with the triumph of good over evil, of life over death!

Then forty days later Ascension Day, bearing its witness to the widening influence of Christian truth as it emerges from a local into a universal faith! Then ten days later, Whitsunday, commemorating the outpouring of the Holy Spirit at Pentecost! Then Trinity Sunday and all the " Sundays after Trinity " calling upon men to worship God in the fullness of His being.

Now that noble outline of lessons and prayers will help to save any minister and congregation from becoming narrow and lopsided. It prevents the minister from playing all of his religious music on a single stop like a bagpipe or all on one string like a jew's-harp. It helps him to become something like a full-toned church organ with its various stops.

It aids him in declaring by his teaching " the whole counsel of God," in place of dwelling all the time upon one or two particular themes which happen to engage his special interest. When we witness the narrowness of certain pulpits, we could wish that some larger plan might be there introduced instead of trusting everything to the subjective impulses and the miscellaneous choices of

John Smith. There is a distinct advantage to be gained by the establishment of a more varied and adequate outline for the instruction and inspiration of the people who represent so many different moods and temperaments, such varied forms of capacity.

In the Prayer Book of the Episcopal Church nothing is left to chance impulse or the extemporaneous output of some man who may, or may not be, possessed of judgment and taste. Here it is in black and white! Here is exactly what is to be said, and all that is to be said, at the baptism of a child or at the confirmation of a believer or in celebrating the sacrament of the Lord's Supper! Here is what is to be said at a marriage ceremony, or in the visitation of the sick, or at the burial of the dead! Here is the proper form of sound words to be used at the laying of a corner-stone, or at the dedication of a church, or at the ordination of a minister, or in family prayer! It is all laid down in systematic fashion so that all may know in advance exactly what is to be said and sung and done. " Decently and in order " — both of these points are strongly emphasized in this branch of the Christian Church.

This constant emphasis upon system and convention is one reason perhaps why this Church does not attract nor develop in its ministry so many men of striking personality as would be the case in other branches of the Church. It does not tend to encourage the development of strong, original and attrac-

71

tive preachers. Phillips Brooks, whose inheritance and earlier training, by the way, were Congregational, was one of the greatest preachers of the Nineteenth Century in this country, but he stood almost alone in his own communion. There was no other preacher in the Episcopal Church in that day to be named with him.

The four clergymen who did so much to make the Episcopal Church strong and useful beyond any other single Protestant church in the city of New York, Bishop Potter and Doctors Rainsford, Huntington and Greer (later Bishop Greer) were none of them extraordinary preachers. They were men of unusual ability in organization and administration. They enlisted the interest of men of large means; they organized a vast body of workers and they pointed the way of advance in serving the spiritual needs of that great city, with the vision of statesmen. All this has high value — it belongs naturally to that branch of the Church which has laid such emphasis upon the value of system in Christian teaching, worship and service.

We find the same principle in their creed statements. In the Baptist Church, as we saw, there are no authoritative creed statements. The Bible is their creed and large liberty is left to individual interpretation. In the Congregational Church each local church formulates and adopts its own creed. But in the Episcopal Church these matters are not left to the judgment of some local church or

of some individual minister. The Thirty-Nine
Articles of Religion, the Apostles' Creed, the Nicene
Creed, and the Catechism tell the Episcopalian
what he is to believe. Here are the articles of his
faith set forth in definite terms all serving to maintain the idea of system and method in religious
conviction! Let all things be done in order, this
church says, in worship, in the reading of the
Scriptures, and in shaping the ideals which are vital
to character. It steadily asserts the high value of
system.

II

This church makes a further distinctive contribution in emphasizing the importance of good taste.
" Let all things be done decently " as well as in
order. Worship the Lord " in spirit and in truth,"
but worship him also " in the beauty of holiness."
Let there be a clear sense of the artistic values in
this spiritual ministry!

God is a God of righteousness, but He is also a
God of grace. He has filled the whole earth with
beauty, — rainbows and sunsets, dewdrops and
twinkling stars, lovely valleys and glorious moun-
tains, as well as wheat fields, potato patches and
apple orchards! In that section of the earth which
is untouched by the hand of man beauty pre-
dominates over utility, — there are many more wild
flowers than there are wild fruits or wild vegetables.
God is a lover of beauty and He has placed deep

within the hearts of His children the capacity for admiration. He has made woman, the very summit of his creation, the loveliest object upon which the eye of man can rest. The leaders of worship in this church call upon the people to worship this Lover of beauty in the beauty of holiness.

The Episcopal Church stands beyond any other for good taste in religion, for decorum in worship and for graceful architecture. The church buildings of no other denomination in the various cities of the land show such good proportions and such fine outlines as do the churches of this faith. The place of worship of an Episcopal church may be inexpensive in some small community, but it will have a churchly look. The exterior as well as the interior will suggest the thought of worship. You will know at a glance that it is not a place to play billiards or to buy groceries or to find a moving picture show. The Episcopal church has set itself resolutely against the habit of fitting up churches with opera chairs or decorating the walls as one might decorate a restaurant or a ladies' parlor in a fine hotel.

All this has had and must have an important influence upon the inner life. It is not a mere matter of æsthetics, it is a matter of devotion. It develops a habit of mind which has immense significance. The Episcopalians do not go to church as a rule so much to hear eloquent sermons or to be entertained by some splendid music — they go to worship and bow down before the Lord, their

Maker. Every one of them has put into his hand at the door of his pew a Prayer Book, indicating that he is there not merely to be preached to, but to pray on his own behalf. And when you enter an Episcopal church any day of the week, Sunday, Monday, Tuesday or Wednesday, you will find there an atmosphere of worship, of aspiration, of yearning for fellowship with the unseen. All this has high value for the development of the religious life.

This habit of good taste shows in their liturgy. These aids to worship are not only systematic, covering almost every conceivable form of human aspiration, they are also beautiful. I have used the Episcopal Prayer Book for thirty odd years intimately and many of its prayers I know by heart. Let a man open his Bible and, as he begins to read, utter that prayer which is appointed for the Second Sunday in Advent: " Blessed Lord who hast caused all holy scriptures to be written for our learning, grant that we may in such wise hear them, read, mark, learn and inwardly digest them that by patience and comfort of thy holy word we may embrace and ever hold fast the blessed hope of everlasting life which thou hast given us in our Saviour Jesus Christ." It puts him in the mood to read his Bible aright.

Let him begin the day, if he will, with that Collect which stands at the beginning of the Communion service: " Almighty God, unto whom all hearts are open, all desires known, and from whom no secrets are hid, cleanse the thoughts of our hearts by the inspiration of thy Holy Spirit that we may perfectly love thee and worthily magnify thy holy name, through Jesus Christ our Lord."

And when he comes to the close of the day and gathers his family around him for evening prayer before they lie down to rest, let him end his devotions with that prayer of St. Chrysostom: "Almighty God who hast given us grace at this time with one accord to make our common supplications unto thee, and dost promise that when two or three are gathered together in thy name thou wilt grant their requests, fulfill now, O Lord, the desires and petitions of thy servants as may be most expedient for them, granting us in this world knowledge of thy truth and in the world to come life everlasting."

We find in these and in other sections of their liturgy the very acme of good taste, the perfection of literary form. The Book of Common Prayer can be set alongside of the King James version of the Bible and Shakespeare. We find also a rich fund of spiritual devotion. When we hear some man praying awkwardly and ungrammatically perhaps, or still worse oratorically, we long for the chaste and reverent simplicity of the ritual. When some man begins to pray and then ceases to pray (although he keeps on talking with his eyes shut, in a kind of general harangue to the Lord about his favorite hobby, presenting arguments for some pet conviction of his own, but losing the sense of direct personal, devout address to God) we wish that he had in his hand some competent guide for his public petitions. I would not advocate the surrender of what is called "voluntary prayer," where a minister voices the needs of those he would lead in prayer in words of his own choosing. Where this is well done I believe its immediate helpfulness may rise above that of all fixed liturgies. But where it is done in thoughtless or slovenly or oratorical fashion, it becomes an offense to taste and conscience alike.

This contribution of good taste is no light matter. We want men to be upright in heart — that lies at the foundation of everything. We want a man to be just, true and clean. But if he is also cultured and well mannered, so much the better! His strength of conviction and his devotion to principle are all very well — we cannot get along without those fine qualities, — but if you are coming into any kind of close contact with him, if you are going to marry him for example, then you would also like to have him well bred and refined.

The Episcopal Church in its whole method of nurture and of culture undertakes to accomplish just that. It says, "Blessed are the gentle, for they shall inherit the earth." It seeks to develop gentlemen and gentlewomen. The saturative influence of good architecture, of tasteful interiors, of good stained glass, where the colors do not eat each other up, of a finely framed liturgy, of noble music and of the spirit of decorum in worship — all this exercises a refining influence upon even the rudest nature which in the course of years of such devotion finds fruitage in qualities of mind and heart which have high value.

This is one reason perhaps why the Episcopal Church has more influence upon the actors and artists of the country than all the other churches put together. The "Little Church Around the Corner" in New York, where so many theatrical people, so many artists and authors have been married and buried, is of course an Episcopal church. The Episcopalians have been more generous patrons of the theatre and of the arts than have been some of the other bodies of Christians, but their mode of worship and their general method are most attractive to those who are constantly striving for the artistic. The Actors Church League has been a great influence for good in promoting higher standards of conduct on the stage. Let all things be done righteously indeed but beautifully and artistically as well! Along this line of good taste, the Episcopal Church has made an important contribution to our total Christianity.

III

This church has also a high sense of the historic values. The word "Episcopal" comes from the

Greek word " *Episcopos*," one who overlooks, oversees, that is to say, a bishop. The Episcopal Church is a church governed by bishops and these bishops attach great importance to what they call " the historic Episcopate." They believe that something of the Episcopate can be traced back through the long history of the Church to the time of the Apostles, that their clergymen are ordained by bishops, who in turn were ordained by other bishops, who in turn were ordained by other bishops, and so on back to the days of Peter and Paul. And some of them, who have the poetic temperament rather than the minds of exact historians, like to think that a certain mysterious grace has been handed down in this way from Christ through his apostles and from his apostles through this long line of bishops to the ministers of that church, rendering them more competent to administer the sacraments than are the ministers of religion who do not stand in this direct line of Apostolic Succession.

It is a lovely picture, interesting if not altogether verifiable. I shall not stop to discuss it, for the purpose of these chapters, as I stated at the outset, is not controversial. I have never been able to find very much about bishops in the New Testament, except in the sense that all their ministers were bishops, that is to say, leaders and overseers of the flock of Christ.

I have never been able to discern any peculiar

or exceptional usefulness attaching to a man merely because he was ordained by a bishop. His usefulness as a minister of Christ seemed to depend upon his physical and his mental, his moral, his social and his spiritual makeup. His efficiency was determined by the measure of his gifts, by the degree of his consecration to God and by the readiness of his sympathy with the needs of his fellows. Oftentimes these fine qualities are possessed by a man who was ordained by a bishop, and just as often — rather more often in fact, because so many more men are ordained by other methods — they are possessed by men who were ordained by groups of elders or by the laying on of the hands of a few fellow pastors.

This sense of historic values leads the Episcopal Church in the United States of America to maintain close and cordial relations with the Church of England. Its bishops attend the Lambeth Conference of Bishops in London. Its clergymen are frequently invited to preach in the pulpits of the Anglican Church. Its first bishops were consecrated by English bishops. Its Prayer Book is modelled after the book of Common Prayer in the Anglican Church. And the Anglican Church has historic relations with the Roman Catholic Church, from which it broke away at the time of Henry VIII. Henry, partly because of his quarrel with the Pope over his domestic affairs, and partly in a spirit of sturdy independence, which had already become a national trait, decided to throw off the rule of the Papacy. Thus the Church of England became independent of the authority at Rome. But through its stately cathedrals and its noble liturgy, both of which are older than the Protestant Reformation, the Anglican Church has kept that sense of contact with the past. And by its close relations with the older Church, the Episcopal Church in America has kept alive that same high sense of historic values.

We find this same sense of a vital touch with the past in its Prayer Book. Here in " The Book of Common Prayer " used in every Episcopal church are the Psalms of Israel, the ancient hymns of the Jewish Church, the finest expressions of the devotional spirit among the Hebrews! Here are the words of Christ and of his apostles in the Gospel and the Epistle for the day! Here are the liturgic forms of the early Church, the Venite, the Magnificat, the Benedictus, the Prayer of St. Chrysostom and all the rest! Here are prayers and collects taken from the Greek and Latin churches of medieval days! Here are choice bits of liturgic expression from the best devotion of all time! The Prayer Book is like a great Cathedral, reaching back to Solomon's Temple and the songs of David, holding within it all those contributions of deep piety, of fervency of spirit and of fine phraseology. When we use it, we join with ancient saints, with the churches throughout the world and with all our fellow believers in humbly and heartily voicing in noble words our common worship of Almighty God.

This high sense of historic values has enabled the Episcopal Church successfully to avoid division in its own ranks. It is a church which is by no means all of one mind. It has its " high church party " and its " low church party " and its " broad church party." But however these men may differ in conviction at many points and in practice at many more, they all manage to move along together in the unity of the spirit and in the bond of peace.

The Methodist Church in this country was divided over the question of slavery. In 1845 it was split into two large churches, the Methodist Episcopal Church and the Methodist Episcopal Church South. These two branches of one great church have remained apart to this hour. They are identical in polity, in their adherence to the Twenty-five Articles of Religion, in the whole spirit and method of their work. They have adopted a common hymnal, so that the two churches sing God's praise Sunday after Sunday out of the same hymn-book. But they remain apart, divided by a question which all but divided our country in those fateful years of 1861-5.

The Baptist Church and the Presbyterian Church were likewise divided over the question of slavery and by sectional strife. But the Episcopal Church, while the meetings of its General

Convention were interrupted during the Civil War, was never divided. When the war was over the General Convention met again in 1865 in Philadelphia, the City of Brotherly Love; the Southern bishops took their places again beside the Northern bishops and everything went on as before. That deep sense of their historic past served to bring all sections together at the close of the war and it has served at all times as a splendid bulwark against the spirit of division.

Here then are elements in that larger faith which have value for us all! The worth of system and method in religious worship and service, the value of good taste and decorum in that refinement of life which belongs to character at its best and that sense of historic values which serves to link us up with all that is good in our past.

In this newer country where so much has been left to ill-considered choices made on the spur of the moment, in this land where rough and ready people, bent upon those material achievements necessary to the development of a new region, sometimes forget all that is due to taste and artistic sense, in this land where everything is fresh and unworn, where the sense of contact with the past is much less felt than would be the case in an older country like England, Italy or France, the Episcopal Church has been performing steadily a high office in the unfolding of our national life.

The Larger Faith

May I speak of yet one other service which the
Episcopal Church has rendered to the people in
this fair land, by the aid she has given in maintaining a warm and real sympathy between that branch
of the English-speaking race which lives on the
other side of the water and that branch which has
its home on this side. Here are two great English-
speaking democracies, put in trust, as we believe,
with certain political and religious ideals, which
have entered vitally into the shaping of our civilization!

There are just two ways for nations to deal with
each other — one is on the basis of military force,
upon the principle that might may usurp the place
of right, and that any nation may undertake to
impose its will upon other nations, if it possesses
the power. That way lies ruin, as we have seen in
these nine fateful years of painful history since the
summer of 1914.

The other method is by the enthronement of
the principle of public right as the governing ideal in
all national and international affairs. It is to this
latter idea that the great English-speaking race
stands openly committed. An imaginary line divides
us on our northern boundary from territory
belonging to the most powerful empire in the world.
More than a hundred years ago we entered into an
agreement with that people that no frowning fort
should mar that boundary line and that no
war-ship from our shores or from theirs should

trouble the peaceful waters of the Great Lakes. The agreement has been scrupulously observed. The great idea of public right enthroned in their hearts and in ours has served to keep the peace and to settle all the differences which have arisen for more than a century. So may it be ever! The Church which has aided mightily in the maintenance of that friendship between those who speak a common tongue and live in a fine sense of agreement as to their moral purposes and political methods, deserves the gratitude of all mankind.

THE LUTHERAN CHURCH

CHAPTER V

The Lutheran Church

We stand at a long remove in miles, in time and in mood from the situation where Martin Luther nailed his Declaration of Independence to the door of the Church in Wittenberg. The main principles which found expression in the Protestant Reformation have to a great extent been taken up into the common consciousness of the modern world. And in making those principles familiar and operative the Lutheran Church has borne a significant and honorable part.

The Protestant Reformation was a great religious movement and it was also in the broadest and best sense political. It voiced a profound dissatisfaction with the existing order which had spread over an entire continent. It involved a sharp break with that mighty organization which had come to dominate in its own interest not only the religious life but the wealth and the learning, the social life and the governments of Europe. It was a movement which called for the coming of a new heaven of religious thought and of a new earth wherein should dwell a finer and less legalistic form of righteousness. It was one of " the days of the Son of Man." Those who had eyes to see saw again the veil of the Temple rent in twain from the top to the bottom.

The Larger Faith

When Protestantism stood up to challenge the right of a mighty system to rule the lives of men, it had emblazoned upon its shield the promise of a new method and a new spirit for all who would fear God and work righteousness. Its four main principles were these:

1. The right of direct and immediate access to God for every soul, with no sort of priestly mediation or ecclesiastical barrier blocking the way. "He is not far from any one of us," and "whosoever will may come."

2. Its doctrine of grace, as opposed to the idea of salvation by penance or by observances or by advances made from some treasury of merit under priestly control or by "works." "By grace are ye saved through faith and that not of yourselves" for Eternal Life is "the gift of God."

3. The authority of the Scriptures — not the decrees of councils, nor the words of popes, nor the traditions of the elders, but the mind of Christ, as it lies reflected supremely upon the pages of the New Testament, was to be the court of last appeal.

4. The right of private judgment, which carries with it by implication all that is contained in our modern program of political and spiritual democracy. Every man by virtue of the fact that he is a man has the same God-given privilege of judging, of interpreting, and of applying these truths of Church and State to his personal needs and to the

needs of the social order, which belongs to every other man.

How full of promise were those four main ideas of the Protestant Reformation! In our day and in our own section of the Christian world they have become the commonplaces of thought and practice. But in that period when priestcraft had successfully overlaid the minds of men with burdens grievous to be borne, the proclamation of these fundamental truths caused the heart to leap.

They made clear the fact that the religion of Jesus Christ is not a mere history of something sacred and beautiful, which happened long ago for our advantage. It is not an elaborate system of artificial observances imposed upon us by external authority. It is not a collection of theories about things quite removed from the daily secular interests of men. The religion of Jesus Christ is a mode of life upon which any soul anywhere may enter immediately by the grace of God for his own eternal good and for the benefit of all those who are touched by the hand of his influence.

The Protestant Reformation stood out also against a false asceticism which had maneuvered itself into a privileged place of sanctity. This was in some measure due to the wholesome humanity of Luther himself who insisted that " the Christian life should be humble and devout but buoyant and joyous," as well. It was due even more to the fact that it took its standards and its spirit from the original source. The gospel of Christ is not in the main a gospel of cutting down and lopping off, a gospel of giving up and of going back to sit down in somber expectation of some better satisfaction in the world to come. The gospel of Christ is a gospel of life. It offers a program and a dynamic for brave, manly, full-fledged, useful, joyous life. " This do," it says, as its Author said at the start, " and thou shalt live." It comes that men may have life and have it more abundantly.

The Protestant Reformation was indeed a " protest " against existing errors and abuses. But it had also its own positive program for the lives of men. It would have said in those days that no man is a Protestant simply because he denies the final authority of the Pope or refuses to attend Mass, or declines the intimate experiences of the confessional. He is only a Protestant when he is putting his full strength into living the life of a responsible citizen in the Kingdom of God, answerable only to his Maker, and sustained by his sense of fellowship with all those who show the spirit of the Master.

Therefore the faith of the Protestant offered to the souls of thousands of men, puzzled and wearied by a system which had brought them neither peace nor strength, a splendid promise of that life which is life indeed. Within fifty years of the time when Luther faced the Diet of Worms it had won a magnificent success. In England and in Scotland, in Sweden and in Denmark, in Prussia, in Saxony and in the Netherlands, it had triumphed. In all the other countries on this side of the Alps it seemed to be on the very edge of victory. It came with all the promise of a new day for northern and western Europe.

How far has that promise been fulfilled in its actual performance? It is a melancholy fact for us that in those first fifty years, Protestantism gained in many sections of Christendom its highest ascendancy. It gained an ascendancy which on divers fields was speedily lost and never again regained.

Its earlier victories over an easy-going, corrupt Church were rapid and decisive. But there came a counter-reformation when the advances of the Protestant faith were checked and held by another quality of church life which had in it the rigor and the vigor of Ignatius Loyola. Then the rapid victories of Protestantism came to an end. And when Protestantism itself became rich and proud, it had no longer its former strength of appeal. As it was in the first century, so it was in the seventeenth, and so it will be ever. It is the movement which is " lifted up from the earth " by discipline and self-sacrifice, which draws men to it.

Many a religious movement has shown itself magnificent in protest, and then has become ineffective when once the protest was accepted and the hour had struck for wise, constructive action.

The Larger Faith

The Unitarian reaction against an impossible orthodoxy and the Christian Science movement as a protest against materialism, have shown themselves strong in criticism — they have not been equally strong in that statesmanship which can develop and carry through large policies of constructive effort.

It was easy for men to draw back from pardons and indulgences, from magical rites and from artificially imposed ceremonies. It was easy for them to insist that bread was bread and wine was wine, over which no priest had any more transforming power than the unordained laymen. But the hard test came when the call was made for that clear-cut, positive, spiritual energy demanded for the renewal and direction of the lives of men and of nations.

No form of religion can live and thrive by what it denies. It can only live and thrive by what it affirms and incarnates. The habit of mind which is critical rather than constructive, the faith which is merely pallid and feeble in the distaste it shows for some of the foods upon which the souls of men are fed, the whole mood which is more intent upon the limitations of its rivals than upon the excellences it can show in its own militant bearing — no one of these is destined to conquer. The negative mood has never been able to hold its own against the highly organized and resolute Church of Rome, to say nothing of winning that harder and more honorable victory in subduing the world, the flesh and the devil.

One of the reasons why Protestantism has not been more successful in fulfilling that early promise is to be found in the fact that it has never been quite brave enough to deal with this human life of ours in its entirety. The Roman Catholic Church, with its seven sacraments reaching out through all the main crises of human life from the baptism of a newborn babe to the last unction for the dying, with its openly proclaimed or covertly held belief in the temporal sovereignty of the Church, with its steady reach for the control of the forces of education and with its confessional projecting the power of the Church into the most intimate relations of daily life, has undertaken the spiritual supervision of man's entire career.

I covet for our Protestant faith some of that same imperialism. I would not see the State or the school, the home or the place of trade controlled by the Church, but I would that all these interests might be brought into obedience to the spirit of Christ. Has the Protestant Church been bold enough to accept for itself openly the entire program of the Kingdom of God on earth? Has it set itself resolutely to the renewal of this entire fabric of civic, commercial and social life after the method of the Master? The saving of privileged souls here and there out of the moral wreck is not enough. The careful nurture of the descendants of those fortunate beings who came over in the *Mayflower*, the habit of attacking human want piecemeal by petty charities, the making of a fair show in the flesh by some hopeful measure of rescue work on mission fields, does not appeal to the moral imagination of the masculine half of the race; and it is losing its power with the more patient part of our population.

Suppose that the Protestant Church for the last four centuries in its hymns and in its prayers, in its sermons and in its lay practice had been standing more clearly for the principle of equality before the law, for a more democratic spirit in the control of our great industries, for a more equitable distribution of the good things of life between those who toil with their heads and those who toil with their hands, for the end of all class legislation and all plundering of the many for the profit of the few, for the banishment of that moral degradation which ensues where the conditions of ill-requited toil become inhuman, for the removal of race prejudice and hatred, and for the development of that quality and measure of national and international morality which would avert war — suppose, I say, that we had been steadily exalting in our Protestant faith that imperialism of the Christ-spirit in all these relations of the common life! Would not our Protestantism today be much further on the road toward the performance of its early promise?

The Lutheran Church

In the Saturday evening editions of many of our metropolitan dailies we find a page given to what is called in bold letters and in pathetic phrase, " The Religious World." Heaven save the mark! As if " the religious world " were a thing apart from the world described on the front page! A thing apart from the life portrayed in the real estate and financial columns, on the pages given to sport, to labor news, and to social events! Where on God's green earth is " the religious world " if not right here where men and women are buying and selling, marrying and being given in marriage, struggling and tempted, broken and beaten in the battle of life!

The man in the street pictures that " religious world " oftentimes as a little toy section of human life off to one side where men of peculiar temperament and dress are busy with their " new moons and their Sabbaths," their incense, and their stained glass, leaving the great interests of justice, mercy and truth in secular life to go their way unblessed and undirected by that spiritual order in whose service those holy men are supposed to stand. In so far as we have allowed our Protestantism to fall into that caricature of its real self, we have no right to expect the performance of its early promise.

I have written thus at length upon the general principles involved in the Protestant Reformation because the Lutheran Church, more than any other single church in this country, has emphasized and perpetuated the prevailing religious attitude in that period of history. "Lutheranism" according to Doctor Henry Eyster Jacobs of the Lutheran Seminary in Philadelphia, "is a mode of viewing and receiving and living the truths of Christianity."

It is differentiated from Presbyterianism which it resembles at many points in polity and method, by being highly Christocentric, to use a technical term, in its theology. Calvinism began with "the divine sovereignty" and through its doctrines of "unconditional election," "effectual calling" and "irresistible grace," worked its way down through the problem of human salvation. Lutheranism begins rather with the joyous experience of the believer in gaining his sense of peace and eternal salvation through his personal faith in and fellowship with Jesus Christ, the Saviour. "Give me John three, sixteen," Luther used to say, "'God so loved the world that He gave his only begotten Son that whosoever believeth on Him should not perish, but have everlasting life,' and all the rest may go." The Lutheran Church rests its whole weight upon the claim that men are saved by grace through their faith in Christ, as opposed to any sort of doctrine which looks toward the securing of the divine favor by "works." The reaction against a widespread and unworthy use of indulgences in the Sixteenth Century produced a deep conviction as to the insufficiency of "works" to secure salvation.

Lutheranism "places no limitations upon the extent of the atonement — it was made not only for all men but for all sins." The only limitation lies in the fact "that some for whom Christ died perish through their rejection of proffered grace."

"Lutheranism knows no priesthood but that of the High-Priesthood of Christ who alone and once for all made a propitiatory sacrifice for us on the altar of the Cross. So intimate is the union between the Saviour and the soul whom He has saved, that there is no room between them for any order of men to conciliate that favor of which the redeemed soul already enjoys the most indubitable proofs."

The very center of its religious confidence and of its manner of worship for the Lutheran is to be found in "the Word of God." By the public and private inculcation of the truths of the Bible, by catechetical instruction and by the generous use of Scripture in its liturgy of worship, the Lutheran Church seeks to make men wise unto salvation and to furnish them thoroughly with impulse and guidance for every good work.

Luther's translation of the Scriptures into German was nothing less than an epoch-making achievement. Translations of the Bible into German had been made prior to that time but having been made from the Vulgate they were in many parts stiff and awkward in their modes of expression. Luther was a scholar in his own right, translating directly from the Hebrew and the Greek — and the style of his translation was idiomatic and readable. He thus rendered a notable and permanent service to the religious life of his country.

The Lutheran Church is a liturgical church and it exalts the value of the sacraments. But it does not allow " the outward and visible sign of an inward and spiritual grace " to interpose itself in any mechanical way between the heart of the Communicant and the Real Presence of the Spirit of Christ abiding within the soul of the believer. " The sole value of a sacrament," Luther taught, " is its witness to the divine promise. It strengthens faith. It seals or attests the God-given pledge of union with Christ and the forgiveness of sins."

In his " History of the Christian Church " the late Williston Walker of Yale University placed this high appraisal upon the work of the man whose name is borne to this day by this great branch of the Church of Christ: —

" Martin Luther is one of the few men of whom it may be said that the history of the world was profoundly altered by his work. Not a great scholar, an organizer or a politician, he moved men by the power of a profound religious experience, resulting in unshakable trust in God, and in direct, immediate and personal relations to Him, which brought a confident salvation that left no room for the elaborate hierarchical and sacramental struc-

5079

tures of the Middle Ages. He spoke to his country-
men as one profoundly of them in aspirations and
sympathies, yet above them by virtue of a vivid
and compelling faith, and a courage, physical and
spiritual, of the most heroic mould. Yet so largely
was he of his race, in his virtues and limitations,
that he is understood with difficulty, to this day,
by a Frenchman or an Italian, and even Anglo-
Saxons have seldom appreciated that fulness of
sympathetic admiration with which a German
Protestant speaks his name. But whether honored
or opposed, none can deny his preëminent place in
the history of the Church."

With the same robust faith exhibited by the man
whose name it bears, the Lutheran Church of our
own day moves out singing with all its strength,

> " A mighty fortress is our God,
> A bulwark never failing."

It inscribes upon its banners those same great
watchwords which have come down across the
ages. Conscious of its direct access to God, heart-
ened to the core by its doctrine of grace, exalting
the Scriptures as furnishing the only true norm of
faith and practice, it seeks to establish its people
for all time in the liberty wherewith Christ has
made them free.

THE METHODIST CHURCH

CHAPTER VI

The Methodist Church

In downright practical efficiency it would be difficult to name a religious leader since the time of St. Paul who would stand higher than John Wesley. He got results, wide, lasting and valuable results.

He came of virile stock — his grandfather had twenty-five children, and his own mother, Susannah Wesley, gave birth to nineteen, John Wesley being the fifteenth. He was a man of culture and scholarship as well as a flaming evangelist. He was a graduate of Oxford and a fellow of Lincoln College. He read the Latin and Greek classics at sight and spoke French, German, Italian and a little Spanish. He was indefatigable in his labors — in his evangelistic tours he travelled over two hundred and fifty thousand miles, far enough to have taken him around the globe ten times. He preached over forty thousand sermons. He was accustomed to rise at four o'clock in the morning and was busy all day, oftentimes far into the night. He lived this strenuous life up to his eighty-fifth year, and when he passed away at eighty-eight he had been preaching with all his accustomed zeal until six days before his death. That is the kind of a Methodist Brother Wesley was, and he has bequeathed a generous portion of his spirit to the largest Protestant denomination in this country.

The Larger Faith

He was not without his limitations — as we travel up and down the world we find men and not angels. The human race has been put ahead in the main essentials of its life by men with hearts in their breasts and with mud on their boots like the rest of us.

John Wesley shared in some of the superstitions of his time. He believed in witchcraft. He believed that hysteria was demoniacal possession. He was accustomed to decide questions by opening the Bible at random and taking the top verse on the page. He preached a rousing sermon, a copy of which I have in my library, on " The Cause and Cure of Earthquakes," — if his diagnosis were correct and his claims verifiable it would have had great value for the city of San Francisco a few years ago.

He felt that many of the events in his own life were the direct results of miraculous intervention, from the stopping of a headache to the cessation of a rain storm, that he might preach in the open air. His familiarity with the Bible was in no sense critical; he had rather a popular or homiletic knowledge of it. But he flung himself into the task of inducing men to forsake their sins and to accept salvation through Jesus Christ beyond any man of his age. He did it with a magnificent success, in which the hearts of all Christian people rejoice. And although he did not sever his own relations with the Church of England, he started Methodism upon its world-wide career of Christian usefulness.

"The Methodist Episcopal Church" is the full name of this branch of Christ's Church. The term "Methodist" was at first a nickname like the name "Christian." It was applied derisively to a group of Oxford students, John and Charles Wesley among the number, because in their determination to deepen their Christian life they lived methodically. They read the Scriptures and prayed and took communion; they visited the sick, the poor, the imprisoned, and performed other acts of Christian service, according to a settled rule and program. They were so exact and conscientious in it that their fellow students called them "Methodists" as distinguished from men who lived by mood and impulse. They accepted the title, and it has come to be the honorable designation of this great branch of the Church.

The "Methodist Episcopal" Church, because it too is governed by bishops, like the Protestant Episcopal Church! The Episcopalians deny the validity of the ordination of the Methodist bishops because the first one was not ordained by a bishop who stood in the line of what they like to call "The Apostolic Succession." But the Roman Catholics in turn deny the validity of the ordination of the Episcopal bishops and their clergy, so the honors are even. The origin of this "historic episcopate" is so lost in the twilight of fable as not to occasion any needful disturbance either in the minds of those who think they have it, or in the minds of those who are perfectly content to be without it.

I

The three characteristic contributions made by the Methodist Church to our total Christianity would seem to be these: First, its splendid Christian zeal. The Methodist Church shows an earnestness and an enthusiasm for the conversion of men, for the enlistment of believers in active service and for the extension of the Kingdom of God in frontier and needy communities beyond any other church. When an ignorant woman heard John Wesley preach, she reported to her neighbors, — " He talks as if he was just dyin' to have ye converted." It was the earnest desire of Wesley to reach the hearts of men and lead them to Christ which led him to break away from the dainty religious essay common to the Anglican pulpit in his day, and to preach without notes in the language of the people, that he might move them by his message. It is that same quality of earnestness which gives fervor and directness to the preaching of the Methodist pulpit to this hour. The church stands as a splendid fulfillment of the Apostolic injunction, " Preach the word; be instant in season, out of season; reprove, rebuke, exhort."

It was their zeal which led them to utilize so largely lay preachers and other untrained men in their early history. Wesley and his followers licensed local preachers and sent them to needy places, where it was impossible to furnish theologically trained clergymen. Their labors have been abundantly blessed. The old circuit rider who went from place to place, preaching in schoolhouses, in the homes of the people, in tents or out of doors, wherever a congregation could be gathered, often had little theological training or literary equipment. He carried a Bible, a hymn-book, a copy of the Methodist discipline, and perhaps a volume of Wesley's sermons in his saddle bags, placing his main reliance upon the sincerity and fervor of his own heart as he called upon men to forsake their evil ways and follow Christ. It was a time when books were not common as they are now, when newspapers and magazines were not in general circulation, and these unschooled men found ready acceptance for their message. They rendered a noble service in laying the foundations of the Kingdom of God out on the frontiers in thousands of neglected communities.

When I speak of " zeal " I do not mean mere noise. There are Methodists who have learned to observe the injunction of the psalmist — " Make a joyful noise unto the Lord." I do not mean mere excitement and hysteria, which are sometimes symptoms of nervous disease rather than of health. I mean that measure of spiritual warmth and desire which shows itself effective in moving and changing the hearts of men. This genuine zeal has borne solid and verifiable fruit. It was one of England's reliable historians who said that in his judgment " John Wesley and the Methodist revival did more to save England from the horrors and excesses of the French Revolution," which worked destruction as well as renewal among their neighbors across the Channel, " than any other single influence which could be named."

In our own country it is widely believed that the work of those circuit riders and pioneer preachers, pushing out into all parts of our land and establishing there the institutions of religion, had much to do with the development of that moral fiber which made our country equal to the exacting demands upon it in the struggles of the Civil War. Lincoln said one day to a group of Methodist preachers who called at the White House to pay their respects to the head of the nation, " The Methodist Church has sent more prayers to heaven for the Union cause and more men into the field and more women into the hospitals than any other branch of Christ's Church." It has been " a zeal according to knowledge " — a knowledge of the human heart and its needs — and it has borne splendid moral fruitage throughout the English-speaking world.

This quality of zeal has tended to develop preaching ability in the constituency of this body. The Methodist Church has produced a great number of effective preachers. Some of these have been notable in the history of our country, — Stephen Olin and John P. Durbin, Bishop Matthew Simpson and Bishop Randolph S. Foster, Bishop Thoburn of India and Bishop William Taylor, a street preacher in San Francisco in '49 and afterward conspicuous for his missionary labors in South America, in India and last of all in Africa. And of men not sufficiently famous to be noticed in history, this church has developed a great number of useful preachers, who, perhaps lacking in the finest literary finish and in the fuller measure of scholarship, have shown, nevertheless, by their practical efficiency in interpreting the Scripture and in bringing help to men, the power of direct and influential address.

The Methodist Church has trusted to the zeal of its clergy, and to the warmth and reality of its own spiritual life, for the maintenance of evangelical faith rather than to any elaborate creed statements or standards of belief. John Wesley abridged the Thirty-nine Articles of Religion of the English Church into twenty-five and these briefer articles have constituted the creed statement of the Methodists since the year 1784. They have never been changed in all these one hundred and thirty-nine years and by vote of the General Conference in 1832 it was made unconstitutional to propose any change in the Articles of Religion. The fact that this creed statement contains only simple, general references to the fundamental articles of religious faith has saved it from becoming an embarrassment to this body of Christians.

The Methodist Church has been troubled little by heresy trials. The earnestness and zeal of the clergy leave them little time for that speculative discussion which often engenders heresy and strife. And it is one of the significant facts of modern church history, that while their standards are broad and simple the Methodist Church throughout the world is in substantial agreement with itself in the substance of its message; and it has remained, through all these one hundred and fifty years, profoundly evangelical in tone.

II

The second contribution lies in its large utilization of the emotional nature in the formation of Christian character. "With the heart man believeth unto righteousness," more than with the head! The main appeal, therefore, should be to the feelings, because people, taking them by and large, do what they feel like doing. They may not reason it all out; they may not make it a matter of strict conscience, but they do certain things or fail to do them because they feel that way. Not a closely reasoned argument on the appropriateness and desirability of Christian life, but the direct appeal to the affections becomes a most useful instrument in the hands of men who would lead others to Christ.

We find this emphasis on the emotional life in

the characteristic warmth and fervor of their preaching. We find it in the greater prominence given to feeling in the hymns of Charles Wesley and of other Methodist hymn writers. We find it in the heartiness of their congregational singing, which is better than that of any other church in America — the people who sing are the people who feel. We find it in the hearty responses in the shape of round " Amens " which sometimes come back from the pew when the speaker has made a telling point. We find it in the outstretched hand and the cordial welcome awaiting the stranger who strolls into any Methodist church.

We find it also in their emphasis upon the doctrine, which they call " the witness of the Spirit." How is a man to know that he has found acceptance with God? " The church will tell him," one group of Christian people says, — " Let him accept the testimony of the church on that point as given from the lips of its priest." " The Bible will tell him," another group replies, — " Let him stand on the promises as made in God's Holy Word." " Let his own reason tell him," others answer; — " if he has met the conditions of salvation, then as a logical result he has found acceptance with God."

No one of these replies would satisfy the followers of John Wesley. " He need not ask the church, or the Bible, or his reason," the Methodist asserts. " God will tell him in his own heart. He will feel

it. The Spirit Himself beareth witness with our
spirits that we are the children of God." The joy
of being saved and of knowing it and of being able
to tell it, has been a leading note in the religious life
of this branch of the Church.

It was a beautiful and a blessed message to bring
to that despondent age to which Wesley preached.
It was a time when the full rigor of Calvinism was
in the saddle and it rode the patient people to their
hurt. It was believed that God by His immutable
decrees had from all eternity determined who should
be saved and who should be lost, and that nothing
that man could do would change those decrees.
The elect would go to heaven, and the non-elect
would go to hell — and that was all there was
about it. This was comforting doctrine to those
who by their own spiritual conceit perhaps, had
decided that they belonged to " the elect." But
as the great majority of people were either too
ignorant or too modest to believe that about themselves, it was a most depressing doctrine. They
had an old hymn which they used to sing:

> " 'Tis a point I long to know,
> Oft it causes anxious thought,
> Do I love the Lord or no,
> Am I His or am I not?"

It all depended upon those " eternal decrees "
which had been established from the foundation of
the world.

The Methodists never sang that hymn. They had no place in their system for any such doctrine. They went everywhere asserting that, " The elect are whosoever will and the non-elect are whosoever won't." They insisted that every man who votes for himself in this matter of salvation is elected. They had not reasoned it all out. They did not undertake to combat on philosophical grounds what the theologians called " predestination," what the man on the street calls " fate," what the scientist calls " determinism." But out of the fulness of their own experience of God's loving mercy, of Christ's offered redemption and of the Spirit's witness to their acceptance in their own hearts, they went about preaching the good news of salvation.

" The Spirit and the Bride say, Come. Let him that is athirst, Come. And whosoever will, let him take the water of life freely." This joyous message touched, and moved, and renewed the hearts of the people, — the Methodist Church grew by leaps and bounds. The joy of their songs, their testimonies, their inner satisfactions became a mighty influence in extending that branch of the Church. " We have not received the spirit of bondage again to fear," they cried, " we have received the spirit of adoption, whereby we cry, Abba, Father."

It would be easy to carry the emotional element in religion to excess where it might result in a useless, unseemly form of self-indulgence. If we should fix our attention solely upon the raptures of religious feeling it might not be easy to distinguish sham from reality. Jumping up and down or shouting so that one can be heard in the next block has no particular value, even where it is done in a religious meeting, unless it leads to something. The final test of anything, feeling, ritual or belief, is conduct, service, life. The Methodist leaders have shown wisdom in undertaking speedily to harness these floods of emotion to some form of practical effort. When this is done the fervor may have great significance. The heart has its rights as well as the head. And in that section of human interest where the two great commandments are not " Thou shalt know " or " Thou shall do," but " Thou shalt love the Lord thy God with all thy heart," and " Thou shalt love thy neighbor as thyself," this emphasis upon the emotional life shows good statesmanship.

III

The third contribution lies in their sense of the value of organization. I regard the polity of the Methodist Church as the best in the world, not even excepting the Roman Catholic. The Catholic Church makes inadequate provision for the growing spirit of democracy. The Methodist polity combines centralized authority, which is entrusted to its general superintendents or bishops, with the spirit of democracy in making large provision for the influence and activity of the laity. It is therefore able to offer a most effective form of church government.

Take this single phase of it — the organization of their ministers into conferences under what is known as " the itinerant system." Every preacher ready for service belongs to some annual conference which covers a certain geographical area. Once a year all these preachers meet together in conference with the Presiding Bishop. The Bishop in consultation with the District Superintendents or Presiding Elders (who have the oversight of smaller groups of churches) appoints those preachers to the places where they shall preach for the next year.

He has absolute power to do this. He could, if he were a man without sense or conscience, entirely override the wishes of any preacher or of any congregation. He may receive information and advice from whatever source may offer, but the final decision rests solely with him. In early days pastorates were limited to one year; then the time limit was extended to two years, then to three, then to five. Now it has been removed altogether, so that a minister may be reappointed to the same church indefinitely, but always for the period of one year. No Methodist minister is ever invited or appointed to the pastorate of any church indefinitely, as would be the case in a Presbyterian or a Congregational church.

The Larger Faith

The system is not without its defects — nothing human is perfect. The only way to have a perfect organization is to prevent human beings from joining it. The system sometimes works disappointment and hardship. A church may not always secure the pastor it wants, or the pastor who would be best suited for it. The minister may not always go where he would like to go and could go. The bishops are not omniscient, but they desire the peace and prosperity of the churches, and they desire the highest usefulness of the ministers. They listen to the suggestions of the laymen who represent the various congregations, they listen to the wishes of the preachers themselves, and then make such appointments as may seem wise and right. And as a matter of fact the system works well. Every Methodist church has a pastor all the time, and every Methodist pastor has a church all the time. There are no discouraging, disintegrating interims when the church is without a minister.

The changes are made on the whole with little friction. The task of getting rid of a minister who has come to be unacceptable to the majority of his congregation is in other communions oftentimes an unhappy experience for him and for them. It may be as painful as having all of one's teeth pulled. But under the Methodist polity when the Annual Conference comes the change can be made quietly, without splitting the church into factions, and without painful embarrassment to the minister. When the Sunday after conference arrives, every church has again its own pastor and every pastor is preaching in his own church. It is a system which works, and that is the best test of any method.

The limiting of the pastorate to short periods in the early history of the Methodist Church enabled it to use large numbers of untrained men, and men of moderate resources, to the glory of God and for the good of society. There is no reason in the nature of the case why a man's ministry in any one church should be of a certain length, five years, or ten years, or twenty years — it all depends on the length of the man. There are men who are "preached out" at the end of a year or two. Both preacher and congregation need what the farmers would call a "rotation of crops." It is an exacting demand which the pastorate of ten or twenty years makes upon a man, standing as he does in the same place twice a week to speak to many of the same people, touching the truths of religion. The wise men of the Methodist Church knew that in the rapid growth of their work and in the absence of a sufficient number of thoroughly trained men, they would be able to use ministers of fewer resources with splendid effect under their itinerant system.

The Methodists have shown a genius for organization. Not content with building up strong churches, they have been fertile in the promotion of more extended efforts. The Chautauqua Movement is non-sectarian, but Bishop Vincent of the Methodist Church was the founder of it, and that church has furnished its largest support. The Freedmen's Aid Society for the education and evangelization of the released slaves has rendered a magnificent service to the nation. The Epworth League, which in numbers ranks almost with the Christian Endeavor Society, as a movement for the training of young people in Christian life and service, is exclusively a Methodist body. The Order of Deaconesses and the Methodist Hospitals in so many of the large cities have given evidence of the same spirit of practical efficiency in this branch of the Church.

By their splendid enthusiasm and zeal, by their wise and wide use of the emotional element in human nature, and by their practical, efficient organization, they have made large and rapid growth in membership until the Methodist Church is the largest Protestant denomination in our country. It was John Wesley who said, " The world is my parish." He meant it intensively, as well as extensively, desiring that the religion of Christ should ally itself with every human interest, as well as spread into all lands. And that body of Christians who revere him as the founder of their branch of the Church has steadily moved ahead in splendid fulfillment of that great hope.

THE PRESBYTERIAN CHURCH

CHAPTER VII

The Presbyterian Church

The claim has been made that " The Presbyterian Church represents more money, more brains and more piety than any other one church in America." It may have no more money per capita than the Episcopal Church, but it is a large church, while the Episcopal Church is one of the smaller churches. It may have no more brains per capita than have the Congregationalists, but it outnumbers the whole Congregational body three to one. It ranks well with any of the denominations in its sense of duty, its attachment to high ideals, and its consciousness of the spiritual world. When we come to add up its material, its intellectual and its spiritual resources, it makes a splendid showing.

The word Presbyterian comes from the Greek word *presbuteros*, which means " an elder." It is a church ruled by elders. The ordained ministers are " teaching elders," and in each congregation there are laymen elected as " ruling elders." The pastor with the elders and the deacons compose the Session, which is the ruling body of the local church. A number of churches conveniently located are organized into a Presbytery, which is made up of all the teaching elders resident within its borders and a ruling elder from each congregation. These Presbyteries are organized into Synods, which oftentimes comprise entire states. Above these Synods stands the General Assembly, made up of ministers and ruling elders in equal proportions, as the highest governing body of the church. The Presbyterian Church is a close-knit, highly organized body standing midway between the monarchical form of church government by bishops, and the pure democracy of the congregational polity.

I

The four distinctive contributions made by this branch of the Church to our total Christianity seem to be these: — First, its spirit of conservatism! It is a cautious, deliberate church. It does not readily lose its head. It is never easy to stampede a company of Presbyterians. They are ready in their own good time to " prove all things," but they are strongly bent on " holding fast that which is good."

They are not likely to go off half-cocked in their hasty acceptance of some new-fangled notion which turned up only last week. It was a fine old Presbyterian pastor who once said of a certain religious pronouncement, "That which is new in it is not true, and that which is true is not new." The Presbyterian Church does not propose to be frightened out of its beliefs because some free lance has had nightmare. It has the conservative habit of mind.

Its three main standards of doctrine are the Shorter Catechism which my own Presbyterian mother taught me in my childhood, the Larger Catechism and the Westminster Confession of Faith. This remarkable Confession was wrought out by an assembly convened in 1643 in England's most famous place of worship, Westminster Abbey. The assembly was made up of one hundred and twenty-one Doctors of Divinity, eleven Lords, twenty Commoners and seven commissioners from Scotland. It continued in session for five and a half years, holding hundreds of meetings. They met every day in the week except Saturday, and sat from nine o'clock until two. Each session was opened and closed with prayer and one day in each month was set apart for prayer, when they came together and continued for four hours in continuous supplication for the blessing of God upon their deliberations. The Westminster Confession thus issued from an atmosphere of earnest devotion.

It was in the time of Bacon and Shakespeare. The King James version of the Bible had just been published. It was a period when the English language was at its best. It was also a time when Christian men were not satisfied with easy-going standards of conduct or superficial statements of belief. The age demanded a creed which would be an impregnable statement of religious truth, to serve as a bulwark against error, as a basis of ecclesiastical fellowship and as an effective instrument for the religious instruction of the people of God. The Westminster Confession came forth in response to that demand.

It is no milk-and-water affair — it is a tremendous document. It undertakes to be the most logical, fundamental and explicit setting forth of man's relations to his Maker anywhere contained in the creeds of Christendom. And when one reads it with an open mind he realizes at once that it is designed to build up a massive and masculine type of piety in the lives of those who give it their adherence.

It is the great digest of Calvinism, the system of that man of iron, who stood forth as a theologian and a reformer in Geneva. It plants itself firmly on the five points of Calvinism. Human depravity — man is hopelessly corrupt and has no power in himself for moral recovery! Unconditional election — God from all eternity has, by His immutable decrees, determined that certain men should be saved! A limited atonement — Christ died for the elect; He did not die for the non-elect, for that would have been shedding His blood in vain! Irresistible grace — in order to make God's decrees of election effective there must proceed from Him a moral influence which cannot be successfully opposed! The final perseverance of the saints — " once in grace, always in grace," for if a man once renewed and numbered among the elect should fall away into sin it would negative one of those eternal decrees. Upon this form of faith, heading up in the " Divine Sovereignty " and dependent for its efficacy not upon the moral preference of the individual, but upon the assertion of an Infinite Will, the Presbyterian churches took their stand.

It would be easy to poke fun at some of the statements of belief included in such thoroughgoing Calvinism — popular novelists, sensational preachers and the secular press have all taken their turn at this interesting diversion. But " by their fruits " we judge statements of belief. These great convictions have empowered men to live nobly and to die heroically beyond those of any other single religious creed which can be named. When spiritual tyranny showed its head in England and in Scotland, in Germany, in France and in Switzerland, men and women of heroic build, fed upon the great convictions of Calvin, stood up to resist and they present a magnificent array of martyrs, who sealed their testimony in their own blood.

It was John Morley, a careful, critical historian, an outspoken agnostic in his own religious attitude, who said: " Calvinism has inspired incomparable energy, concentration, resolution. It has exalted its votaries to a pitch of heroic moral strength that has never been surpassed. They have exhibited an active courage, a resolute endurance, a cheerful self-restraint, and an exulting self-sacrifice which men count among the highest glories of the human conscience." It is impossible for any thoughtful man to dismiss such a system with a sneer.

It was John Fiske, the philosophical historian, standing himself on the border between Unitarianism and agnosticism, who paid this tribute to the sturdy influence of Calvinism upon the cause of human freedom:

" It would be hard to overrate the debt which mankind owes to Calvin. The spiritual father of Coligny, of William the Silent, and of Cromwell must occupy a foremost rank among the champions of modern democracy. In the presence of the awful responsibility of life, all distinctions of rank and fortune vanished; prince and pauper were alike the helpless creatures of Jehovah and suppliants for his grace. Calvin did not originate these doctrines, but in emphasizing this aspect of Christianity, in engraving it upon men's minds with that keen-edged logic which he used with such unrivalled skill, he made them feel, as it had perhaps never been felt before, the dignity and importance of the individual human soul. It was a religion fit to inspire men who were to be called upon to fight for freedom, whether in the marshes of the Netherlands, or on the moors of Scotland."

The Presbyterian Church has taken that theological system known as Calvinism and has held on to it with a tenacity which amazed the Nineteenth Century, and will amaze this light-hearted

Twentieth Century, accustomed as it is to say that it does not care what a man believes, if only he is sincere. The Presbyterian Church cares. It is a doctrinal church, doctrinal in its preaching, doctrinal in the tone of its periodicals, doctrinal in requiring theological soundness in its office bearers. From candidates for admission to the membership of the church it requires nothing but repentance for sin, faith in the Lord Jesus Christ and the consecration of the life to God — it is exceedingly simple and broad as to its doctrinal requirement. But from its ministers and ruling elders it has required, until recently, assent to the entire Westminster Confession, and even now its demands are more exacting than those of any other Protestant denomination.

We would naturally expect that the most famous heresy trials of the Nineteenth Century would occur in the Presbyterian Church. Robertson Smith of the University of Aberdeen, one of the most gifted students of the Old Testament in modern times, was deposed from his chair for heresy. David Swing of Chicago, one of the most thoughtful and popular preachers in that busy city, was compelled to leave the Presbyterian Church because of heresy. Professor Charles A. Briggs of Union Seminary was excluded from the Presbyterian Church for teachings which seemed to conflict with the Westminster Confession. Professor Henry Preserved Smith of Lane Seminary, Cincinnati, was similarly deposed, and the agitation regarding Professor (now President) A. C. Mc-Giffert, of Union Seminary, made it seem appropriate to him voluntarily to withdraw from the Presbyterian denomination.

Where conservatism does not spring from narrow-minded bigotry or from sheer obstinacy, we honor it. Personally I could no more believe some of the statements in the Westminster Confession than I could believe that two and two might make five. But here is a large, thoughtful, conscientious body of Christian men and women, who do believe that these statements are true and because of their loyalty to conviction they are prepared to accept whatever difficulties may attach to insistence upon these standards.

In the everlasting struggle for human progress we need the conservatives no less than the liberals and the radicals. We need those men who, by their very habit of mind, will be sure not to abandon anything that has value. We need those who, revering the great accomplishments of the past, are ready to bring out of their treasures things new and old — the old as well as the new. And in these days when great numbers of people do not know what they believe or why they believe it, it is of great significance that we have this sturdy, faithful, conscientious body of Christians bent on holding fast all that has shown itself good.

II

The Presbyterian Church has kept alive a profound sense of the enormity and the ill-desert of sin. This church takes the moral life of the race seriously. It has never fallen into the way of thinking of evil as only " good in the making " or of saying that wickedness is only " one of the growing pains of virtue." It would have no sympathy with that popular preacher of London who claimed that " the drunkard reeling through the streets in brutal fashion is after all only engaged in a mistaken quest for God." It does not believe that the sinner will naturally and easily grow up out of his sin into the goodness of a saint by a process of evolution. It believes as the apostle did that " men have given themselves up to uncleanness through the lusts of their hearts; that they have become vain in their imaginations and their minds have become darkened; that they have changed the truth of God into a lie and that the wrath of God is revealed from heaven against all ungodliness and unrighteousness." The Presbyterian Church has the sense of sin.

Have any more terrible batteries ever been turned upon the wrong-doing of the world than those of Calvinism! When certain sections of the Church were granting indulgences on easy terms, allowing men to clear up their moral accounts with the Almighty by paying thirty cents on the dollar;

when other leaders were insisting that the waters of baptism would instantly wash away whatever stain or corruption might cling to the moral nature; when others were speaking gently of the evil in the world as a kind of childish aberration, the Presbyterian churches were steadily insisting that sin is an act of rebellion against rightful authority; that it is an insult and an outrage to the love of a holy Father; that it is a heinous and fatal corruption of the nature, to be cured only by supernatural grace and divine redemption.

The chief end of man, as they view it, is not to have a good time or to cultivate one's own powers or to " evolute " into his own completer self — " The chief end of man is to glorify God and enjoy Him forever." At the very beginning of that finer quality of life which is not self-centered, but finds its center in the Divine will, there must come an open recognition of one's sinfulness. The prodigal who comes back from the far country must say first of all, " I have sinned and am no more worthy to be called thy son."

Is there not cause! We often put rubber tires on the words we apply to evil in these comfortable days, lest some evil doer should receive shock or jolt. Lying is only " prevarication "! Stealing is " an unfortunate kleptomania "! Lust is only " the unschooled throbbings of nature " according to many a modern novel. Graft is not civic treachery and crime, as it once was — it is " one of the exigencies of business life under the intricate conditions of modern industry."

If we should keep on mixing our colors, by and by nothing would be wrong! We should have neither black nor white but only a few indistinct shades of gray. And when nothing is wrong, when the power of hating evil is lost, then the race will become morally bankrupt. All honor to that branch of the Christian Church which has maintained its keen sense of the ill-desert, the enormity and the infamy of sin against God!

The wholesome effect of this attitude has been witnessed on many fields. You may recall the austere morality of Cromwell's Army, unparalleled in the military annals of the world. Army life is often a school of vice; it becomes the crucial test of morals and religion. But the army of Ironsides became the wonder of the world for its moral purity no less than for its intrepid valor. They marched against the most renowned battalions of Europe, chanting their psalms and relying upon the Unseen God — and somehow they seemed never to fail in destroying whatever opposed them. It is the testimony of Macaulay, of Goldwin Smith, of John Morley and of other historians, who touch upon that period of history, that no army has ever so combined heroism and purity.

" In that camp no oath was heard, no drunkenness witnessed, no gambling seen. The property of man and the honor of woman were alike safe.

No servant girl was compelled to mourn by the rough gallantry of these red-coats. Not an ounce of plate was stolen from the shops of the goldsmiths." All this from Macaulay's " History of England "! Taine adds, " They raised the national morality even as they had saved the national liberty! " This was an army of Calvinists, taking Scripture texts for their watch-words and countersigns, singing the hymns of the faith as their battlecries! They cherished a profound sense of the malignity and the hatefulness of sin, and thus they trampled temptation under their feet even as they put their enemies to flight.

III

The third contribution of the Presbyterian Church has been its devotion to the Bible. No other denomination has surpassed it in attributing, as the result of painstaking scholarship, such unique and final authority to the Bible. The head and front of Dr. Briggs' offending was not so much that he taught that the Pentateuch was composed of many and sometimes conflicting documents, or that the book of Isaiah was the work of more than one man! It was that he claimed in his famous address that there were three sources of authority in religion — the Bible, which was the classic utterance of the mind of the Lord in literature; the Church, as the utterance of the Divine Spirit to be found in the great consensus of human

134

experience and testimony throughout the ages of Christian history; and Reason, the noblest faculty in man acting at its best in pronouncing upon the validity of the claims of religion. The Bible, the Church and Reason were concurrent sources of authority according to Dr. Briggs; and this exaltation of two other sources of instruction to the place where they would share in the unique honor accorded the Bible became to a large number of Presbyterians insupportable.

This exaltation of the Bible by the Presbyterians has not been merely a traditional and sentimental attitude. The Presbyterian Church has been distinguished from the first for painstaking and profound scholarship. The Westminster Confession is not made up of a lot of pious, well-meaning, but ill-considered platitudes — it is painfully and rigidly learned. The Presbyterian Church has had great doctors of the faith — the Hodges and the Alexanders of Princeton, Shedd and Schaff, James McCosh and Francis L. Patton, Roswell D. Hitchcock and Marvin R. Vincent, Francis Brown and Benjamin B. Warfield. They were men who had studied the subject; they were competent to speak. They knew exactly what they believed and why they believed it, and were not to be badgered out of it by the flourishes of a few popular novelists or the flings of some newspaper reporters, who, theologically speaking, did not know their right hands from their left. Out of this learning came

those scholars who with one accord exalted the
Bible for its inspiration and final authority.

We may not hold with these men in all their views
but that attitude gave an impetus to Bible study.
It lay at the root of the strong insistence of the
Presbyterians upon high standards of ministerial
education. The Presbyterian Church has shown
itself unwilling to ordain men without college and
seminary training. This exaltation of the Bible has
promoted a thorough ands ystematic study of the
Scriptures in their Sunday schools and in the homes
of their people. It has encouraged all the members
of the church to strive to understand and rightly
divide these words of truth which are the final
source of authority in all matters of faith and
practice. In these days, when critical study and
the purely literary treatment of the Bible have been
unsettling the faith of many and have been lower-
ing the Bible in the estimation of others, this
supreme honor placed upon the Word of God by
this branch of the Church has been of inestimable
worth.

IV

The Presbyterian Church has stood strongly for
the value of an intelligent Christian nurture.
One might indicate a certain difference here by the
words " crisis " and " process." The sacramental
idea of religion makes much of the crisis — the
unbaptized individual is unregenerate, but holy

water in the hands of an officiating priest applied to the child or to the believing adult will enable him to pass from death unto life. The emotional type of religion makes much of the crisis — if there can only come an overturning, overwhelming crisis in the feelings of the individual, then in that hour he may enter upon a regenerate life.

According to the other view, religion is to be phrased rather in terms of domestic life, the Father bringing up His children gradually into conscious, obedient, joyous fellowship with Himself. It may be phrased likewise in terms of education, the Master of our spirits leading His disciples, pupils, learners, into self-realization by self-expression in worship, in service and in fellowship with Him. Here salvation is a moral process, conducted by the Spirit of God in the hearts of teachable men.

The Presbyterian Church makes much of this. By thorough religious instruction in the homes of its people, it aims to hold its children within the power of Christian nurture. It maintains that the ideal is for the child never to know the hour when he does not live in the love and the service of God. Family discipline, family prayer, the instruction of children in the catechism and the maintenance of the offices of Christian nurture in the home have been of unspeakable advantage to this branch of the Church. Its course of action has been a lesson and an example to Christian people of all communions. It has often held aloof from the sudden, startling modes of awakening religious interest. It places its emphasis upon the quieter and in the long run the more reliable modes of Christian nurture for the extension of the Kingdom.

This church has rendered a noble service in the history of our country. It has had great preachers of the gospel of Christ — John Hall and Theodore Cuyler, Howard Crosby and Charles H. Parkhurst, Henry van Dyke and William P. Merrill, John Kelman and Henry Sloan Coffin, in a single city! These honored and useful pastors by their strong preaching and their winsome personality have made a lasting impress upon the life of that restless, populous city of New York.

This church has written a noble record in the work of Home and Foreign Missions — Jessup, Thompson and Bliss in Syria, John G. Paton in the New Hebrides and Sheldon Jackson in Alaska, and many other men highly honored in the field of Christian effort! It has reared up a splendid body of intelligent, conscientious and influential laymen. When we call the roll of Presbyterian presidents, senators and jurists, we find it a long and worthy roll of honor. By its conservative temper, by its sense of the awfulness of wrong-doing, by its devotion to the Bible, and by its emphasis on the Christian nurture of the child, it has made a distinct and valuable contribution to our total Christianity.

THE ROMAN CATHOLIC CHURCH

CHAPTER VIII

The Roman Catholic Church

" There never was on this earth a work of human policy so well deserving of careful study as the Roman Catholic Church. Its history joins together the two great ages of human civilization. No other institution is left standing which carries the mind back to the days when the smoke of sacrifice arose from the Pantheon at Rome and lions leaped upon their victims in the Coliseum. The proudest royal houses of Europe are but of yesterday compared with the long line of Supreme Pontiffs in the Vatican. The Roman Catholic Church was great and respected before the Saxon had set foot in Britain, before the Frank had crossed the Rhine, when Greek eloquence still flourished in Antioch, when idols were still worshipped in the Temple of Mecca. And the Roman Catholic Church may still exist in undiminished vigor when some traveler from New Zealand shall take his stand on a broken arch of London Bridge to sketch the ruins of St. Paul."

These are the words of Thomas Babington Macaulay, one of the most widely read historians of the English-speaking race. He wrote them in his famous essay on Von Ranke's *Lives of the Popes*.

141

The Larger Faith

Make full allowance for the showy rhetoric which rendered him more admirable as a brilliant essayist than as a careful, accurate historian, we still have here a judgment which causes every serious man who reads it to reflect! The Roman Catholic Church, as a world-wide, age-long, highly organized institution must be reckoned with in every land on the globe. However we may agree or disagree with some of its doctrines, here is a mighty force in human affairs, not only ancient and august, but at this very hour tremendously vital and significant!

I have not space here to discuss its long and varied history. I have not time to consider its many doctrines, of which it has more and to us as Protestants, more incredible ones, than any other branch of the Christian Church. I shall not undertake to indicate all of the points at which I personally would dissent from its positions touching the work of public education, the place of civil authority or the intellectual attitude to be maintained toward Modernism in philosophy and religion. It would take a long time to do that with anything like thoroughness and the purpose of this little book is not controversial. I would not widen but lessen the gulf which hinders the various branches of Christ's Church from sympathetic coöperation touching the great main interests of character and service. I feel much as did a celebrated Englishman when he returned from several years of service in India where he had been aiding in the introduction of a better educational system — " I have lived too long," he said, " in a land where people worship cows to make much difference in my treatment of those who worship Christ in different ways." I am writing these pages in the hope that I may help some of my fellow Christians to understand each other better.

The four main contributions which the Roman Catholic Church has made to the larger faith in my judgment are these:

I

First, the inculcation of the habit of worship! All church people worship God, but Catholics, we may say not irreverently, have " the habit " beyond any other body of Christians to be named. The little children as soon as they are able to toddle up the aisle of the church, to cross themselves with holy water and to bow before the altar, are steeped in the habit of worship. When they become men and women they feel moved to go to church, not to listen to some eloquent sermon — they may not know who is to preach, or that any one is to preach — not to enjoy an elaborate program of attractive music, but to kneel before the Lord their Maker and offer to Him the adoration and allegiance of their hearts.

Every Catholic church stands open all day and every day in the week, inviting the passer-by to come in and worship. When one enters there may be no service of any kind in progress, but there are the symbols of the Christian faith, there is an atmosphere of reverence and devotion and there will commonly be found a group of his fellow beings stopping to unburden and refresh their hearts in personal worship.

One summer when I was in Italy I visited the great cathedral at Milan just at sunrise. As I passed into that magnificent temple visited every year by tens of thousands of people coming from the ends of the earth to stand silent and awestruck before the dignity and beauty of its architecture, I saw just outside the door a dozen huge market baskets. They were filled with produce, lettuce, spinach, radishes, onions — the market women who owned the baskets were on their way to market to sell the products of their gardens. And then, as I reverently moved up near the altar, I saw these old peasant women to whom the baskets belonged. Their faces were bronzed, scarred and wrinkled by hard work and exposure. They had stopped for a few moments on their way to work to worship. And these rough, shabbily dressed market women felt thoroughly at home in that magnificent cathedral. No one save an American Protestant would have thought of giving them a curious glance. And when they arose from their knees and passed out, they had gained a feeling of spiritual refreshment, a new consciousness of the greatness of human life even under the rudest conditions, an

144

added sense of their kinship with the Eternal in whose honor that costly temple of worship had been reared. And that habit of worship is wonderfully and beautifully established in the sentiments and the practice of a great mass of people, more than two hundred millions of them, who confess allegiance to the Roman Church.

It is a vast service to render. It is especially significant in an age which is deficient in its attitude of reverence, in its sense of the unseen and in its readiness to fall down silent and expectant before the Most High. You may go through the streets of any city in Christendom and you will see early on Sunday morning crowds of people on their way to worship. In most cases no special announcement of the service has been made in any public way through the newspapers or otherwise, but the people are on their way to the house of God because of this ingrained habit of worship. Masses are held at six o'clock, seven o'clock, eight o'clock, nine o'clock, ten o'clock and congregations of people attend them. You will find them there in their pews, on their knees, with their lips moving in prayer. They are listening for a voice from heaven to speak peace to their souls. I question seriously whether this settled habit of worship can be matched in any other branch of the Christian Church.

The Larger Faith

The second contribution this church has made may be found in the habit of obedience to authority. " Poverty, chastity and obedience " — these are the three radical vows taken by an army of men and women in the Catholic faith. They renounce all claim to private property, receiving only a bare support. They " belong to the Church " in a very real sense, to be used by the Church as may seem to it wise and good. For the sake of the service which they have undertaken, they refuse the sweet joys of family life. It is desired by their church that they should be free from all domestic responsibilities so that they can go or come as their superiors may direct. And obedience, prompt, unquestioning, unmeasured, to the head of the Order to whose service they have dedicated their lives, has become for them the rule of life. This obedience on the part of great numbers of monks, nuns and priests of various orders has its influence upon the entire body of Catholics until that idea of obedience to authority has become a leading note in their religious life.

Now I might not choose that for myself — I am frank to say that I would not — but I am not so blind as to fail to recognize the immense spiritual value it may have in service rendered to the Kingdom. Thank God for the Roman Catholic Church! Some of its doctrinal positions, — its belief in the infallibility of the Pope, in the power of priestly absolution from sin, in the idea of the actual sacrifice of Christ in the service of the Mass, in its belief in the real presence of the body and blood of our Lord in the bread and wine of the sacrament, in its conception of Purgatory — it would be impossible for me to accept. I am opposed to every sort of encroachment by ecclesiastical authority, either Catholic or Protestant, upon the exercise of that civil authority which in a democracy like ours belongs to all people alike. I am opposed to any interference by church authorities with the work of public education. But while I differ with my Catholic friends at many points in my philosophy of the State and in my convictions touching theological truth, I thank God for the immense moral and spiritual influence of that great church.

We have not in these days so many effective moral forces in the world that we can afford to think lightly or to speak harshly of any of them. When we find a mighty organization exercising an influence, which it is not easy to estimate, upon the life of the race, making for reverence toward God, for that righteousness of life which comes from obedience to his commands and for the prevalence of spiritual ideals, we may all find here an occasion for gratitude.

The Catholic Church has at this moment under its care and direction vast numbers of comparatively untaught people in Italy, in Spain, in Austria,

in South America and in Mexico which we as
Protestants simply would not know what to do with
if they were all suddenly to renounce their loyalty
to the Catholic Church and proclaim themselves
Protestants. We have here, in this more enlight-
ened and freer country, vast numbers of people in
our cities, who are better cared for in their present
state of development and with the temper it has
pleased God to give them, under that system which
teaches obedience to authority, than they would be
under that mode of church life which happens to
be my own.

Take it in the service it has rendered at one
particular point, the matter of sobriety! The
Catholic Church has not seen fit to take official
action, as the Methodist Church and some other
churches have done, throwing its entire influence
upon the side of the prohibition of the manufacture
and sale of intoxicants. It has had in its membership numbers of men who were engaged directly or
indirectly in the liquor business. In most of the
Protestant Churches of America you would find
none at all, because such men would be refused
membership unless they made a change in their
business. The Catholic Church in the United
States has in its membership great numbers of
people who grew up in foreign lands where the
whole custom of using alcoholic drinks as a beverage
is very different from the custom which has pre-
vailed among most of the church people in this land.

It is responsible for those people who are under its care, to be guided into something better.

But it has in its priesthood any number of men who by virtue of that habit of obedience to authority have rendered a great service for good in the lives of rough men and women to whom intemperance is a real peril. In my last parish my near neighbor and good friend Father McNally of St. Patrick's Church, was an active, enthusiastic member of the Father Matthew Total Abstinence Society. He went about among his people, brought up many of them under very different surroundings from those which I have known from my childhood, urging upon them by precept and by personal example the Christian duty of abstinence from the use of intoxicants. He accomplished in hundreds of cases what no Protestant clergyman could ever have accomplished under the conditions where he worked. This has to do with but a single virtue. In keeping alive also the sense of a world unseen, in promoting the feeling of moral obligation, in causing men to know that there is open to us all a definite source of help to aid us in our struggle, the unique authority of the parish priest among his people has a value which we would be sorry to lose from the moral forces of the community.

In mediæval times it was this spiritual authority of the Catholic Church which alone showed itself mighty enough to subdue the turbulent elements in society, to put a certain check upon military tyrants and to infuse something of the spirit of mercy into those who would otherwise have been the ruthless oppressors of their weaker fellows. And today in great sections of our modern world the same work is being done in other terms and under other conditions — spiritual authority holds in check certain evil forces before which less autocratic methods might find themselves helpless.

In these three directions particularly one can see this power at work: it sets itself over against that materialism which is no closet theory but a base mode of life; it sets itself against the revolutionary type of social agitation which would burn and slay in order to gain its ends; it sets itself against the spirit of unrestrained self-indulgence, a wild and reckless Bohemianism which fears neither God, nor man, nor devil. The Roman Catholic Church stands with a brave front lifting up before the people in picture and in statue, in anthem and in prayer, in public sermon and in the words of the private confessor, the nobler ideals of the Son of God. We are not far enough along toward the Millennium to wish to break in pieces that vessel of honor even though, to some people, it may seem to contain so much of wood and of earth. The gold and the silver of precious spiritual influence are there.

The length to which this spirit of obedience will go almost passes our Protestant belief. The story of the Jesuits, that powerful Order founded by Ignatius Loyola, reads like a romance. The spiritual forces of Protestantism have been likened by one writer to "local militia, useful for defence in case of invasion, but incapable of being sent abroad for the purpose of spiritual conquest." Rome has her militia in a vast number of ordinary parish priests in all lands, but she also has her standing army, made up of forces ready at a moment's notice to be sent upon any foreign service however distant or disagreeable or dangerous.

If it is believed at headquarters that a certain Jesuit father in England or America would, because of his talents or character, be particularly useful among the Hottentots of Africa or the Bushmen of Australia, or the Eskimos of the frozen north, the next week he will be found sailing to that quarter of the world, the next month he will be preaching, catechizing and saying Mass among those same surroundings. The Roman Catholic Church develops that spirit of obedience to authority which is at once a menace where it is unworthily used, or a mighty prophecy of spiritual achievement where it is directed to worthy ends. " Whatsoever he saith unto you do it " — this was the word of Mary, the mother of our Lord, to the servants at the wedding in Cana of Galilee. It is in that atmosphere of prompt and unquestioning obedience that water is turned into wine.

The Larger Faith

III

The third contribution made by the Catholic Church lies in its promotion of the spirit of trust in the unseen. The Roman Catholic Church meets the human soul at the very threshold of its earthly experience and offers to provide some satisfying measure of spiritual direction for every crisis. This is the meaning of its seven sacraments, where the Protestant Churches have but two.

Here is Baptism for the new-born babe, the stated recognition of his spiritual kinship with a great body of aspiring souls in the Church, and of his kinship with the Father, Son and Holy Spirit, into whose triune name the child is baptized.

Here is Confirmation for the child when he reaches the age of personal, moral decision and is ready to stand before the world as a professing Christian, prepared to take his first communion.

Here is the sacrament of the Lord's Supper, the bread and the wine transformed, as they believe, by the words of consecration into the veritable body and blood of the Saviour so that the inner life of the communicant may feed upon Him and become like Him.

Here is Penance, where the soul in the confessional relieves itself by breathing the story of its moral failure into the ear of a trusted and merciful friend, gaining for itself, through the assurance of human forgiveness an added confidence in the divine forgiveness, and having prescribed for it certain acts of devotion or of service to be rendered as an offset to the wrong done.

Here is the sacrament of Orders, the formal setting apart of a man to a life of religious devotion, that he may become a leader, a priest and a mediator of spiritual values to his needy fellows.

Here is Marriage, the union in the name of God of one man and one woman for life; and all honor to the Roman Catholic Church for its steadfast and consistent opposition to the inroads which hasty and easy divorce has made upon the sanctity and the integrity of the home! The Catholic Church regards marriage as an earthly copy of the mystical union between Christ and His Church.

Here at the very end of one's career is Extreme Unction, where the soul is finally prepared for its solemn and mysterious journey into the unseen world.

Now all these seven sacraments become to the devout Catholic, outward and visible signs of an inward and spiritual grace. At all the important crises of his life and touching all its more vital interests, the church places before him these symbols of an unseen economy of divine mercy and help. By the perpetual recurrence of these rites in the appointments of his church, the believer may be maintained in that attitude of trust which gives him peace.

In these practical days when so many people are

inclined to believe only in those things which can be seen with the eyes, handled with the hands, or purchased with money, when the things that are seen and temporal so often expel from our vision those unseen things which are eternal, it is good for one branch of the Church steadily to inculcate by methods which have shown themselves effective, an abiding trust in those intangible aids which mean so much in the gaining of that more abundant life to which we are called.

No other church has made so much of that supreme manifestation of the divine mercy toward sinful men witnessed on Calvary. The Catholics go to Mass. Good Catholics make all manner of sacrifices and subject themselves to all sorts of inconvenience rather than refrain from going to Mass at least once every week. The Mass is a visible enactment and repetition of the sacrifice of Christ on Calvary, according to their belief, offered in atonement for man's sin. These worshippers go there to commemorate afresh the death of the Son of God and to confide afresh in the great mystery of divine redemption there proclaimed. On every altar and in many a Catholic home there is the Crucifix. The Stations of the Cross (those pictures which are found in every Catholic church), indicate the stages in Christ's progress from the judgment hall of Pilate to Calvary. Now the divine mercy revealed on Calvary may be to the Jews a stumbling-block and to the Greeks foolishness, but it is the power of God unto salvation to every-one who trusts. The Roman Catholic Church has made a most important contribution to "The Larger Faith" by its promotion of the feeling of trust in the great fundamental offers of the Christian gospel.

IV

The fourth contribution it has made lies in the marvelous readiness of its faithful members for sacrifice. This fine quality of life is present in all Christian churches but the Roman Catholic Church can show an unusual measure of it. It faces every man toward the demand for a sacrificial life.

The Pope has a palace. He lives in the Vatican at Rome, which is a spacious building, containing, we are told, more than ten thousand rooms. These rooms are filled with the treasures of art, with great libraries of books, and with the necessary appoint-ments for the physical comfort of a large household, but the Pope has no home.

The priests have their clergy houses but not a man among them has a home. It takes a woman, a wife and a mother with her children to make a home. And ruling out the unfaithful priests to be found, alas, in every branch of the Church, there is in the Roman Catholic Church a great body of pure and true men who have surrendered the hope of all these joys that they might give themselves in sacrificial fashion to the service to which they are called.

The Larger Faith

It is the very jewel and crown of a woman's life to love and to be loved by her husband and children, to busy herself with the furnishing and the ordering of a home. But here is a vast company of sweet-faced, quiet-voiced, pure-hearted women surrendering all that for the sake of the service to which they give themselves. Sisters of Charity, Sisters of Mercy, Little Sisters of the Poor, and all the rest! Here they are, the teachers of youth, the friends of the aged and the helpless, the faithful nurses of the sick and the sympathetic helpers of the outcast! Like the Son of Man, they go about doing good.

We see them daily on the streets of every city in Christendom. Whenever I pass two of them, I feel like lifting my hat. Here they are, the messengers of the divine purpose in sacrificial service! They are the followers of Him who came, not to be ministered to but to minister and to give His life for the ransom of many.

Have you ever read Francis Parkman's histories, with his account of the work of those early Jesuit fathers among the Indians of our own country, and of Canada? Have you read the story of Father Damien, among the poor lepers of Hawaii, upon the Island of Molokai? Have you read the record of Pere Marquette's work among the red men in the Northwest and of Junapero Serra among the Indians in California? The noble self-sacrifice of it has written a record that brings again before us the

moral heroism of Apostolic Christianity. " I, if I
be lifted up from the earth, will draw all men unto
me," said One who knew what was in man, and
needed not that others should tell him. It was his
own sober estimate upon the power of sincere love
for the souls of men and of the habit of uncom-
plaining sacrifice on their behalf. Whatever may
be one's feeling touching some of the beliefs and
some of the forms of the Roman Catholic Church,
we will all agree that it has made a splendid showing in that heroic and beautiful self-sacrifice which
suffereth long and is kind, which beareth all things,
believeth all things, hopeth all things, endureth
all things.

I write as a Protestant minister, but I am sure
that I voice the sentiments of hundreds of thousands of my fellow Protestants when I say that we
would like to cultivate closer and more friendly
relations with this ancient and far-reaching branch
of Christ's Church. They are our brethren in the
Lord. Both they and we are striving for the coming
of the Kingdom of God on earth, which means the
sway and rule of the divine Spirit of righteousness,
peace and joy, in all the affairs of men. I am confident that the pastor of many a Protestant church
would be happy to welcome to his pulpit one of the
faithful priests of the Roman Catholic Church to
speak to his people the words of eternal life. He in
turn would be glad to speak in any Catholic
Church to which he might be invited, not to change

the Catholics into Protestants, but to help them by his message to be more faithful and useful members of the church of their choice.

We are glad that in this land of freedom and democracy the relations in many communities between the Catholics and Protestants are to such an extent filled with the spirit of our common Master. The influence of such broad-minded Catholics as the late Cardinal Gibbons of Baltimore, and Archbishop Ireland of Minnesota, and other men of like spirit, has aided greatly in this happier relation. May their number increase! We are all grateful for the habit of worship and for the spirit of obedience to rightful authority, for the sense of trust in the unseen, and for the capacity for self-sacrifice which this great church has contributed in generous measure to our larger faith.

The Catholic Church has been imperial in its ambitions and in its methods, as would befit an organization which heads up in Rome. I covet for this larger faith, made up of the varied contributions of these many branches of Christ's Church, that same imperialism. Not that I would see the State or the public school, the home or the place of trade ruled by any ecclesiastical organization. God forbid! But I would that all these institutions should be brought into obedience to the spirit of Him who is the Head of all the Churches. Would God that all these churches in their several ways might set themselves, not to the mere saving of privileged souls from the general moral wreck! Would God that they might set themselves to the great task of the moral renewal of man's entire life in its social, economic and political relations! All these kingdoms of human interest and action must some time become kingdoms of that mode of life for which Christ stood. It is for us all to take hold together " in the unity of the spirit and in the bond of peace " to achieve that sublime result.

THE UNITARIAN CHURCH

CHAPTER IX

The Unitarian Church

The doctrine of " the Unity of God " is much older than William Ellery Channing. It is much older than the Arians of the Fourth Century who stood up to resist the stout orthodoxy of Athanasius in the Council of Nicea. Abraham, Isaac and Jacob, Moses, David and Isaiah were all Unitarians in their thought of God. The vast Moslem world, whose faith at its inception was a vigorous protest against the weak idolatry of the Orient, is to this hour a world of Unitarians — " There is no God but Allah, and Mahomet is His prophet." We find a multitude of Old Testament saints, of Moslem believers and of thoughtful men in all periods of religious history, who would stand together in saying, " To us, there is but one God, the Father."

But Unitarianism in its more restricted sense, as applied to a certain branch of the Christian Church, dates back in this country to about the year 1815. Early in the Nineteenth Century a very considerable group of Congregational churches in New England separated themselves from the Orthodox wing of the denomination which still held to the general system of belief known as " Evangelical." In Boston every Congregational church except the " Old South " joined in this new departure. They retained the Congregational form of polity and in most cases the historic names and the meeting houses where they had been accustomed to worship.

The separation came as a thoughtful, conscientious reaction against some of the excesses and some of the teaching connected with " the Great Awakening." Reason and conscience alike protested against such doctrine as that found in Jonathan Edwards' terrible sermon on " Sinners in the Hands of an Angry God." The time was ripe for some radical modification of the religious teaching which had become traditional with the orthodoxy of New England and the Unitarian movement was the clearest and most influential expression of that demand.

The liberal party was not large numerically. The Unitarian denomination today is still one of the smaller sects. It is a party to be weighed rather than counted. But it has registered a profound and wholesome impress upon the religious belief, upon the literature, upon the philanthropy and upon the civic purposes of the Nation. No one who understands its early history and the real quality of the men who gave direction to its development in those days will speak slightingly of the Unitarian Church.

I

The main contributions which it has made to

our total Christianity seem to me to be, First, its steady insistence upon a reasonable faith! In those early days when the most rigorous form of Calvinism was to the fore the Unitarian movement had also its " five points," but very different points they were from the five points of Calvinism.

1. It stood for the universal Fatherhood of God. " To us, there is but one God, the Father," they said, and all these legal, forensic, mediatorial schemes of salvation must either square themselves with that fundamental fact or they must stand aside.

2. It stood for the real humanity of Christ. In their insistence upon his divinity the orthodox party had at times obscured the fact that whatever else Christ may be, He was a man, born of a woman, tempted in all points like as we are, subject to the laws of growth, of pain and of death. The Unitarian stood for the actual humanity of Christ, not a mask, nor a pretense, but a genuine humanity which tasted the human situation to the full for every man.

3. It insisted on the religious function of history, not only Hebrew history, but all history, as a revelation of God. The Unitarians boldly affirmed that God has not left himself without witness in any land or in any age.

4. It placed the Bible at the center of a vaster revelation of the mind of the Lord through literature — the relation of the Bible to other books of

spiritual worth being germinal rather than exclusive of their claims to some measure of inspiration.

5. It insisted that salvation is a moral process conducted by the Spirit of God in the lives of thoughtful, obedient and aspiring men — a moral process, not a legal, mechanical or magical transaction, imputing man's guilt to an atoning Saviour or imputing the righteousness of Christ to unrighteous men by some sort of theological shuffle. It was a moral process in which the Spirit of the living God utilizes not only dogma and sacrament but other agencies, as well, which may contribute to the development of character.

Here are five points — the Fatherhood of God, the humanity of Jesus, the function of history as a revelation of God, the germinal relation of the Bible to a vaster body of sacred literature and the conception of salvation as a moral process — all of them reasonable, all of them scriptural, all of them helpful! They have been so far accepted by the more intelligent and open-minded branches of the Church as to seem to many of us commonplace, but time was when it cost many a man the affection and confidence of his associates in Christian effort to insist openly upon these five points of a reasonable faith.

It was a protest sorely needed. The Unitarians stood out against a doctrine of the Trinity, which often implied three distinct Gods. They opposed a view of Christ which slighted his humanity in the interests of a certain plan of salvation. They condemned that narrower view of history which left great sections of human interest outside the pale of God's love and care. They put their strength against that conception of salvation, which represented it as something outward, legal, mechanical. They refused to set religion in conflict with the intelligence and moral wealth of the world where these were found not allying themselves with the theological positions of Calvinism. As George A. Gordon of the Old South Church, Boston, pointed out, their protest at these points was "tremendous, magnificent, wholesome." It was reason and conscience in such wise and godly men as Channing and Dewey, Theodore Parker and James Freeman Clarke, William C. Gannett and William H. Furness arraying themselves against certain theological claims which were neither reasonable nor moral.

It was therefore an ethical no less than an intellectual protest. It would be difficult to name two men in the Nineteenth Century in whom the moral sense was more keenly alive than in William Ellery Channing and James Martineau. It was the spiritual passion of their own great, warm hearts which moved them to defend the character of God against the unworthy implications put upon it by some of the orthodoxy of their day.

Certain theories of the Atonement represented God as only allowing His anger against faulty men

The Larger Faith

to be appeased by the sufferings of Christ, upon whom the full penalty of the guilt of the whole world was visited — it was a frightful doctrine, unwarranted by the teaching of the Four Gospels. The claim was made that God in determining from all eternity by an unconditional election that certain men should be saved was under no obligation to respect our rights or interests — this notion seems to most of us preposterous. Read some of the current religious literature in the last half of the Eighteenth Century and you will understand how some of the choicest spirits this country has ever produced went out from the larger orthodox body of Christian believers, impelled by reason, by a truer knowledge of what the Bible actually teaches, and by the impulses of their own honest hearts.

It was a protest overdone in some instances — when the pendulum swings it often swings too far. In the minds of certain people God the Father became grandfatherly, the thought of moral rigor and disciplinary purpose in His attitude toward men was obscured. In some minds " the dignity of human nature " was such that man did not need a Saviour, did not need forgiveness, renewal, and strengthened purpose in order to attain. To some light-hearted people all literature was so full of what they were pleased to term " inspiration " that it did not matter whether men's minds were ever fed upon the great conceptions and aspirations

of David and Isaiah, of John and Paul, or of our
Lord Himself — Shelley and Walt Whitman,
H. G. Wells and Bernard Shaw will suffice. These
friends speedily reveal the fact that they have been
reared on spiritual gruel altogether too thin to
make them morally robust.

But the Unitarian movement is not to be judged
by its worst but by the main trend and drift of its
influence upon the religious life of the Nineteenth
Century. It was, at its inception, an emergency
movement shaped up with reference to the necessi-
ties of a specific historic situation — it has continued in a substantial way and it has made good
its protest in the more reasonable and more scriptural positions held today by almost all of the
churches of Christ.

When we come to view it as a movement of
thought and life, we find that Unitarianism represents not so much a body of churches as " an
individual way of looking at the facts of life and its
problems." It is said that " Boston is not a place
on the map — it is a state of mind." There is
truth as well as humor in that epigram. If some
sort of chemical analysis could detect the " traces "
of the wide influence of those men and women
who for the last two hundred and fifty years have
been speaking and writing in and around Boston,
we would all agree that Boston is a very useful
" state of mind." In like manner Unitarianism is
not so much certain columns of figures in the Year

The Larger Faith

Book where religious statistics are compiled —
Unitarianism is " a state of mind," an individual
way of looking at the problems of life which is
characterized by reasonableness.

The influence of this way of looking at things
can be discovered in the entire religious life of this
nation. Thousands of people who once walked in
darkness have seen a great light. Only a small
percentage of them have been enrolled as Unitarians, but the more winsome, reasonable and
creditable message of religion, to which the influence of this small denomination has so largely
contributed, has won their hearts to an open allegiance to Jesus Christ. Even the Salvation Army,
with its " blood and fire " methods and theology,
is a nobler institution today, because it lives and
works in a land where Emerson and Channing,
Lowell and Longfellow have spoken to the mind and
conscience of the nation.

The kingdom of heaven in some of its manifesta-
tions is " like the growth of a grain of mustard
seed," an outward, visible, organized expression
of a finer quality of life. The kingdom of heaven is
also " like leaven," silent, pervasive, contagious,
gradually leavening the whole lump and thereby
rendering it more palatable and useful in meeting
human need. The emphasis of the Unitarian upon
the reasonableness of religious faith has been like
leaven.

II

The second contribution made by this denomination lies in the breadth of its culture. When it claimed that all history had a function as a revelation from God, it summoned the intelligence of the race to stand in the presence of all lands and of all ages as on holy ground, putting the shoes from off its feet as it listened everywhere for accents of the divine voice. When the Unitarian insisted that the Bible was preëminently the sacred book, but that all literature worthy of the name might have some breath of the divine and share in that sacredness, he gave a new impetus to the interest which thoughtful, devout men might feel in the best that has been said in literature. It has been characteristic of this branch of the Church to stand for a noble breadth of culture.

It has produced men of letters in numbers out of all proportion to the size of the denomination. " Thou Bethlehem of Judea art not least among the provinces," for out of thee has come a movement of mind which has exercised a renewing influence upon the thought of our entire country! How many of the noblest names in our literature are the names of Unitarians! Ralph Waldo Emerson was the pastor of a Unitarian church in Boston. Lowell and Longfellow, Bryant and Holmes, Nathaniel Hawthorne, Frances Parkman and George Bancroft, William H. Prescott, John Lothrop Motley

171

and John Fiske, Charles Eliot Norton and Thomas Wentworth Higginson were all Unitarians.

Lyman Beecher, a war-horse of orthodoxy, once said — " All the literary men of Massachusetts are Unitarians. All the trustees and professors of Harvard College are Unitarians. All the elite of wealth and fashion in Boston crowd the Unitarian churches." They have, in the last hundred years, produced a royal company of seers and of singers whose messages of insight and uplift have made us all their debtors. It would be difficult to name any other single influence upon our youth, emanating from an American mind, which has counted more or counted for better things than the writings of Ralph Waldo Emerson.

It was a Unitarian who founded the " Lowell Institute " in Boston, an endowed lectureship so well maintained that from fifty to one hundred lectures are offered free every winter, delivered by eminent men in this country, and oftentimes by men from Europe. In my own college days there I heard James Russell Lowell give six lectures on the " Early English Dramatists." I heard Richard S. Storrs lecture in his matchless way on " Bernard of Clairvaux," and Theodore Roosevelt lecture on " Civic Reform." The service of this nobly endowed lectureship to the community can scarcely be overestimated.

It was a Unitarian who generously endowed the " Boston Symphony Orchestra," which by his ample provision became the first organization in this country to present, in a manner which ranks with the best in Europe, the great musical compositions of the masters of melody and harmony.

It was a Unitarian who founded " Cooper Institute," in New York, which through its popular appeal and the variety of its activities has become one of the most useful institutions in that mighty city in leading the thoughts of the plain people to higher things. It has been characteristic of the Unitarian denomination to stand for breadth of culture, believing that into the redeemed life of the race, " the kings of the earth," the leaders and masters of the higher human values, should " bring their glory and their honor " as into a city that lieth four-square.

III

The Unitarian Church has been conspicuous for its contribution of a wise interest in philanthropic effort. This has been no cold-hearted, technical skill in dissecting the problems of poverty and crime, of civic wrong and social injustice. Some of the mightiest of the reformers have sprung from this branch of Christ's Church, bearing with them the moral passion no less than the wise judgment which belongs to this denomination at its best.

The men and the women who waged the earliest battles for the abolition of human slavery recruited their ranks in large measure from the Unitarian

The Larger Faith

churches. Channing himself, and Theodore Parker, who made Music Hall in Boston a modern Forum for the voicing of the public conscience; Charles Sumner and Wendell Phillips, Gerritt Smith, Samuel J. May, and Julia Ward Howe were all of them Unitarians.

In more recent times, in dealing with vice and crime, in meeting the demands which the charities and the corrections of the country are making upon brain and heart, there are few more honored names than those of Edward Everett Hale and Samuel J. Barrows. I was a visitor for the Associated Charities in Boston thirty-five years ago, and at that time more than half the money and a great deal more than half the time and wisdom and love spent in personal service in that humane effort came from that denomination, although it is one of the smaller branches of the Christian Church. If one should appraise the Christianity of any group of people by the showing they make in embodying in their lives the spirit of the Good Samaritan or by the standards named in that judgment scene portrayed in the twenty-fifth chapter of Matthew — " Inasmuch as ye have done it unto the least of these, ye have done it unto me " — he would find the Unitarians meeting that test in satisfying measure.

It has been a broad-minded philanthropy. It was Dr. Samuel G. Howe who gave impetus and direction to an awakening sentiment in Massachusetts for the more efficient care of the blind. The Perkins Blind Asylum, where Laura Bridgman and Helen Keller received their training, sprang out of his efforts. It was Horace Mann who led the way in broadening the scope of education, making it include Manual Training for boys.

It was Edwin D. Mead who, more than any other single man in our country, aroused that sentiment which opposes increased armaments and urges the reference of international differences to properly constituted international courts as a substitute for the barbarous, burdensome habit of war. It was Charles F. Dole who was a leader in the work of scientific temperance agitation, bringing to bear upon the menacing evil of the rum shop, the best judgment and largest experience of the nation to replace the inefficient and intemperate zeal of certain reformers who only serve to cloud the issue. It was George T. Angell who aroused the pity of the country for dumb animals and led the movement which resulted in the organization of " a society for the prevention of cruelty." In every form of philanthropic effort you will find the intelligent heads and the warm hearts of Unitarians bearing an honorable part.

In civic affairs the Unitarians have rendered notable service. The people of California will never forget the debt of gratitude they owe to Thomas Starr King, pastor of the First Unitarian Church, San Francisco, for the far-reaching influence he exerted in helping to save California to the Union, and enlisting her on the side of the struggle for the liberty of all men. Some of the noblest men we have had in the councils of our nation have been men of that faith — Charles Sumner and Senator Hoar, John Hay, John D. Long, William Howard Taft, and many others whose names would fill a worthy roll of honor! The movement for Civil Service Reform was greatly indebted for the advancement of its interests to individual members of this church and to the organized utterance of the church itself along that line. George William Curtis, Thomas Wentworth Higginson, Charles W. Eliot, and many another honored citizen stood up to resist the idea that " to the victor belong the spoils " — they insisted that " a public office is a public trust."

Piety and patriotism should go hand in hand. When intelligent Jews prayed for the peace of Jerusalem, they did it both as citizens and as churchmen, for Jerusalem was the capital of their country, as well as the site of the temple. And in the Unitarian branch of Christ's Church there has been throughout an intelligent insistence upon the sacredness of civic life and the importance of those duties which belong to citizenship in the Republic.

" One God, the Father " — ours no less than theirs! Many of us cannot accept the estimate they place upon the person of Christ, nor agree with certain views they hold touching other matters which seem to us vital. With all the gratitude I feel for the service they have rendered, I could not be a Unitarian. But even so, we may well believe that the agreements are more significant than the differences. We have been told on the highest authority that the vital thing in religion is not the ability to say, " Lord, Lord! " but the doing of the will of the Father who is in heaven. In that day many obedient, aspiring souls, who have differed widely in their theological interpretations, may come, moved by one common desire to live in the vision and service of the highest they saw, to sit down with Abraham and Isaac and Jacob in the kingdom of God.

"THE UNITY OF THE SPIRIT"

CHAPTER X

"The Unity of the Spirit"

In somewhat cursory fashion, with no pretense
of thorough, exhaustive treatment, we have passed
in review certain distinctive contributions made by
these various branches of the Church to that larger
Christianity in which we all believe. We have been
happy to find in other denominations elements of
strength and points of excellence which were not
equally conspicuous in our own denominations.
We are glad that these varied notes are being struck
by men of different moods and temperaments, by
men of different tradition and training, to the end
that a fuller, richer volume of worship and of service
may thereby become possible. Let each man stand
up in his own chosen place and say with gladness of
heart, " Other sheep He has which are not of my
fold — them also He will bring, that at last there
may be one flock and One Shepherd."

We have gained in these days a generous supply
of " religious tolerance " — we are not fighting
our fellow Christians in other camps as misguided
men have done in the past. But tolerance is not
enough. The very word " toleration " smacks of
offense. I am not happy in having any one " toler-
ate " me and I should feel myself an insufferable

prig were I to assume an attitude of " toleration " toward any fellow Christian. We must have insight, understanding, appreciation.

We can engage in the pleasant, harmless custom of holding " Union Thanksgiving services " together when the last Thursday in November comes but has the Twentieth Century of Christian history nothing better to show in the way of Christian unity than that? We need to exchange " the poor charity of mutual forbearance " for " the benign consciousness of inward sympathy and active coöperation."

In the smaller communities in this country the struggling rivalry of the churches sometimes crowds out the usefulness of the Church. If we had fewer churches we would have more Church. As Dean Hodges once said, " Effective blows are not struck with extended fingers, but with the solid fist. We may threaten the devil with the Baptist finger or the Methodist finger, with the Roman Catholic finger or with the Episcopal thumb, and he faces the assault with great serenity; but when our total Christianity comes to make an undivided assault, he may be led to meditate upon retreat." We may in our differing taste as to ritual and polity, in our varying interpretations of the eternal mystery, be as distinct as the fingers of the hand. But we may also in that suggestive and useful variety be so knit together and held within the power of a common passion for righteousness, that, in a splendid "unity of the Spirit," we shall go forth to conquer.

This finer and firmer unity will not be attained by an arbitrary suppression of differences, but by the fuller development of the distinctive contributions which each branch of the Mighty Vine of Christian organization is making to the aggregate result. "Sink deeply into the inmost life of any Christian faith and you will touch the ground of them all." The city that hath foundations is surrounded by walls great and high, but they are pierced by many gates of entrance, three on every side. When we enter that city of God, we shall find that the various guests of the divine bounty, though fed at separate tables, have all been fed upon the same bread of life and their lips have all been touched alike with the same wine of remembrance.

"There is a tide in the affairs of men which taken at the flood leads on to fortune." In that world-wide struggle for justice, for freedom and for democracy in which we are engaged in these strange, hard days, the leaders of our Christian forces might well discern the flood-tide of opportunity! We see the whole race passing through a profound historical transformation. We see the current methods of social and political organization challenged to justify themselves by the measure of well-being they can show in the lives of men. There is opened unto us everywhere a wide and effectual door for moral advance. In all this we as Christians are meant to have a large and honorable part.

In such a time of stress it is difficult to be patient toward that spirit of sectarianism which blocks the way. The unity of Christendom seems of less importance to an ecclesiastical dyspeptic than does the fact that he and his wife, his son John and his wife, should be privileged to live under a form of church polity and usage, constructed in strict accordance, as he maintains, with some obscure passage (wrongly interpreted as often as not) in the Book of Acts. In the presence of the dire need of the whole earth for spiritual direction at the hands of those forces for which all the churches profess to stand, many of these petty differences in theological theory and in denominational practice become as trivial as the fact that some good men have and some good men have not red hair. The minister of Christ who spends his time on Sunday defending his own particular mode of baptism, or expounding some notion of Biblical inerrancy to the discomfiture of those " higher critics " against whom he thunders, or exploiting some special theory of future punishment, is not even fiddling while Rome is burning. He is not doing anything as respectable as fiddling. In the presence of whole continents on fire such a waste of time and of sacred opportunity is downright wicked.

We learned, as never before, in those fateful years of war how much larger the local unit, the national unit, or the international unit must be if it would reach its highest efficiency in military action. The local militia held apart from any vaster force of resistance or attack showed itself all but valueless. It took the organized and disciplined forces of whole nations banded together and acting in concert to achieve the necessary ends. How much longer will it take for the children of light to realize that the local and the national units in that vaster, nobler Army of God must likewise be made larger if they would win?

Christianity is not today the mighty cable it was meant to be, binding the nations to the Throne of God. It has been frayed out into so many strands that no single thread or group of threads has in it the necessary fiber for the strain which that high task would impose. We are not in our several communities, nor in the nation as a whole, in a position to furnish that competent and impressive moral leadership which the complex life of this modern world sorely demands.

We need above all else, save only the gracious enduement of the Holy Spirit, that wise and patient leadership which will federate these scattered forms of effort into an imposing and achieving unity. We need the firm grasp of mighty leaders — not Bismarcks, who by sheer strength of the churchly equivalents of " blood and iron " might weld these rival states of denominational life into an empire strong enough to defy the world. The mind of Von

185

The Larger Faith

Moltke was not the mind of the Master. We need rather religious statesmen with the temper and skill of Abraham Lincoln, who " with malice toward none, with charity for all, with firmness in the right as God gives them to see the right," will guide these sectarian states out of their rivalries into that willing coöperation which would produce an imperishable republic of God. That would be Christian union indeed, and that type of union would hasten immeasurably the coming of that Kingdom in which all Christians believe.

The stronger metals can only be welded together or moulded into nobler forms when they are at white heat. When the metal is cold it resists and breaks. In like manner there are human institutions, vast and weighty, which can only be recast when the material out of which they are formed has been brought to white heat. In these grave times when the whole world is in the crucible, may it not be that God is calling upon us for a new alignment, a better formation and a more complete mobilization of all our spiritual forces for the great task of world redemption? The dire need is summoning all the members of the body of Christ to show that they are one body in Christ, ready to act together in a finer concert of power.

We have so often associated the word " Catholic" with the Roman adjective that multitudes of unthinking Protestants are afraid of it. Would that it might be recovered to its rightful use throughout the world! "I believe in the Holy Catholic Church" and I belong to it. I pray for the gathering up of all these fragments of the body of Christ into the Holy Catholic Church.

It doth not yet appear what form this Christian unity shall take. No one can say just how this comprehensive action of our Christian forces may be secured. Personally I do not believe that it will come by an amalgamation of all the religious bodies of the world into one vast, all-embracing ecclesiastical organization. The unity of Christendom will not be outward and mechanical — it will be "the unity of the Spirit in the bond of peace." But we know that in proportion as He appears in all our corporate religious life, the net result will be like Him.

These are wonderful years and there is much to be done. The world has been torn to pieces by a great disaster — it will have to be rebuilt and built better than it was before the War. Let Christianity stand up straight — the ceiling is high! Let it make bare its arms — there is hard work ahead! Let its eyes sweep the whole horizon — the field of opportunity is the world! Let it make bold to attempt the moral renewal of the life of the race — nothing less than that will satisfy Him whom we serve! Let it go forward in "the unity of the Spirit" to write chapters in its future more glorious than any in its past!

The Larger Faith

" Build thee more stately mansions, O my soul,
 As the swift seasons roll!
 Leave thy low-vaulted past!
 Let each new temple, nobler than the last,
 Shut thee from heaven with a dome more vast,
Till thou at length art free,
Leaving thine outgrown shell by life's unresting
  sea!"

APPENDIX

Appendix

When the substance of these chapters was used in a series of evening addresses in the United Church of New Haven, Connecticut, the three hymns sung at each service were selected from hymn writers belonging to the particular denomination to be considered that evening.

It is an interesting and significant fact for the cause of Christian unity that these many hymns, written by members of these different communions, were all contained in the Hymnal, " In Excelsis," in use in the church where the addresses were given — as indeed they would be found in almost any standard hymnal. Doctrinal discussions may divide us, but we all come together in prayer and in praise.

The list of these various hymns may be of interest to those who read this book. It does not contain any hymns written by the " Disciples of Christ." Excellent hymns have been written by members of this communion but being more recent it did not chance that they were included in the Hymnal in use at that time in United Church.

The Larger Faith

BAPTIST.

> Softly fades the twilight ray.
> I need Thee every hour.
> Blest be the tie that binds.

CONGREGATIONAL.

> My faith looks up to Thee.
> I love thy kingdom, Lord.
> O Master, let me walk with Thee.

EPISCOPAL.

> O Little town of Bethlehem.
> The Church's one foundation.
> For all the saints who from their labors rest.

LUTHERAN.

> A mighty Fortress is Our God.
> O Sacred Head, now wounded.
> Now thank we all our God.

METHODIST.

> Love divine, all love excelling.
> Jesus, Lover of my soul.
> A charge to keep I have.

PRESBYTERIAN.

> I heard the voice of Jesus say.
> Go labor on, spend and be spent.
> Stand up, stand up for Jesus.

ROMAN CATHOLIC.
> Lead, Kindly Light.
> Jesus, Thou joy of loving hearts.
> Jerusalem the golden.

UNITARIAN.
> Lord of all being, throned afar.
> In the Cross of Christ I glory.
> Nearer, my God, to thee.